Margaret Skinnider

✦

HISTORICAL ASSOCIATION OF IRELAND

LIFE AND TIMES

NEW SERIES

General Editor: Ciaran Brady

Now available

Margaret Skinnider

MARY McAULIFFE

Published on behalf of
the Historical Association of Ireland
by

UNIVERSITY COLLEGE DUBLIN PRESS
Preas Choláiste Ollscoile Bhaile Átha Cliath
2020

This first edition published 2020 in collaboration with the
Historical Association of Ireland by
University College Dublin Press

ISBN 978-1-910820-53-7
ISSN 2009-1397

University College Dublin Press
UCD Humanities Institute
Dublin 4, Ireland
www.ucdpress.ie

Cataloguing in Publication data available from the British Library

Typeset in Scotland in Ehrhardt by Ryan Shiels
Text design by Lyn Davies
Printed in Dublin on acid-free paper by
SPRINT-Print, Rathcoole, County Dublin, Ireland

CONTENTS

Plates section between p. 78 and p. 79

FOREWORD

Originally conceived over a decade ago to place the lives of leading figures in Irish history against the background of new research on the problems and conditions of their times and modern assessments of their historical significance, the Historical Association of Ireland Life and Times series enjoyed remarkable popularity and success. A second series has now been planned in association with UCD Press in a new format and with fuller scholarly apparatus. Encouraged by the reception given to the earlier series, the volumes in the new series will be expressly designed to be of particular help to students preparing for the Leaving Certificate, for GCE Advanced Level and for undergraduate history courses, as well as appealing to the happily insatiable appetite for new views of Irish history among the general public.

CIARAN BRADY
Historical Association of Ireland

For the women in my family who were members of Cumann na.
mBan in County Kerry
1918–22

*

My Grandmother
Johanna 'Jo' McAuliffe (née O'Connor),
Secretary, Duagh Cumann na mBan

My Grand Aunts
Josephine 'Josie' Nolan (née Kennelly),
Ballydonoghue Cumann na mBan
Mary 'Minnie' Mulcaire (née O'Connor),
Duagh Cumann na mBan
Mary 'Mamie' Ahern (née O'Brien),
Ballylongford Cumann na mBan

ACKNOWLEDGEMENTS

I would like to thank Ciaran Brady and the Historical Association of Ireland for this opportunity to contribute to the Life and Times Series. Thanks are also due to UCD Press editors Noelle Moran, Conor Graham and Ruth Hallinan for their guidance and advice. As always I am indebted to the friendships and networks among historians of Irish women's and gender histories in Ireland, in particular my friends and colleagues in the Women's History Association of Ireland. The WHAI provides many of us with a home and a platform for our work. I am also indebted for the support of my colleagues in Gender Studies in UCD, Associate Professor Ursula Barry and Dr Aideen Quilty.

I am very grateful for all the help and support from the librarians and archivists in the National Library of Ireland, University College Dublin Archives, the archives of Kilmainham Gaol, Trinity College Dublin Manuscripts, the Burns Library, Boston College, the Glasgow Women's Library, and the Military History Archives of Ireland. I am also indebted to Stephen Coyle in Glasgow, as well as Mackie Rooney, Patsy Brady and all members of the Margaret Skinnider Appreciation Society in Monaghan and to Fergan O'Sullivan, Margaret's nephew. I wish to express a special thanks to Margaret's grandniece, Janet Wilkinson, whom I first met when I was the historical consultant on the RCSI 2016 commemorative exhibition of the 1916 Rising. Janet kindly shared the archive she has, of Margaret photographs, with me. I would also like to thank Robert O'Keeffe, grandnephew of Nóra O'Keeffe, for sharing his family memories of Nóra with me.

Thanks to Dr Margaret Ward, Dr Maggie Feeley, Dr John Borgonovo, Dr Leeann Lane, Dr Sinead Kennedy and all who encouraged me to write about Margaret. Thanks, as always, to my family, my mother Nancy, my brothers, sisters, and my nieces and nephews, who were their loving, supportive and teasing selves, always listening to me go on about the women of the 'auld Cumann na mBan'. In particular I owe a huge debt of gratitude and an expensive dinner out to my sister Bridget, who proofread the manuscript. And of course, as always, heartfelt thanks to Julie, for her constant love, support, and encouragement.

MARY McAULIFFE
January 2020

ABBREVIATIONS

ASU	Archive Service Units
BMH	Bureau of Military History
CEC	Central Executive Council of the INTO
CPC	Central Propaganda Committee
DORA	Defence of the Realm Act
DMP	Dublin Metropolitan Police
FOIF	Friends of Irish Freedom
GHQ	General Headquarters
GPO	General Post Office
ICA	Irish Citizen Army
ICTU	Irish Congress of Trade Unions
IHA	Irish Housewives' Association
ILP	Independent Labour Party
INAA	Irish National Aid Association
INAAVDF	Irish National Aid Association and Volunteer Dependents' Fund
INTO	Irish National Teachers' Organisation
IRA	Irish Republican Army
IRB	Irish Republican Brotherhood
ISW	Irish School Weekly
IVDF	Irish Volunteers Dependants' Fund
IWSLGA	Irish Women's Suffrage and Local Government Association
IWWU	Irish Women Workers' Union
LPC	Lower Prices Council
MSPC	Military Service Pension Collection
NDU	North Dublin Union

NUWSS	National Union of Women's Suffrage Societies
RCC	Republican Reconstruction Committee
RCSI	Royal College of Surgeons
SAC	Strike Administrative Committee
SPI	Socialist Party of Ireland
UVF	Ulster Volunteer Force
WAC	Women's Advisory Committee
WPI	Workers Party of Ireland
WSPL	Women's Social and Progressive League
WSPU	Women's Social and Political Union

CHRONOLOGY OF SKINNIDER'S LIFE AND TIMES

1892
Margaret Frances Skinnider is born on 28 May in Coatbridge, Scotland.

1910
A Sluagh (Branch) of Na Fianna, the Irish Boy Scouts' Association, is founded in Glasgow by Joseph Robinson

1912
Skinnider becomes involved in the militant suffrage campaign in Glasgow.

1913
Skinnider graduates from Notre Dame Roman Catholic Training School for Teachers.

1914
Skinnider joins the suffrage protests outside of Perth Prison in July.

1915
In April Skinnider joins the Anne Devlin Branch of Cumann na mBan in Glasgow. During Christmas 1915, Skinnider brings explosives to Countess Markievicz in Dublin.

1916
Skinnider joins the Irish Citizen Army Garrison at St Stephens Green on Monday, April 24. Wounded three times during a sortie, she is operated on by the Cumann na mBan First Aid women. In December, she travels to America on the *SS California*.

1917

Skinnider joins several Republican women, including Hanna Sheehy Skeffington, Nora Connolly, Nellie Gifford and Min Ryan, on propaganda speaking tours across America. She publishes her memoir *Doing My Bit for Ireland* (New York, 1917).

1918

In July Skinnider returns from America with Nora Connolly and Hanna Sheehy Skeffington on the *Matagama*, which sails to Liverpool.

1919

Skinnider and Nóra O'Keeffe, her lifelong partner, return to Dublin and set up home together in Fairview. Both join the Fairview branch of Cumann na mBan.

1920

As well as her Cumann na mBan activities, Skinnider continues to be a member of the Irish Socialist Party, the Irish Women's Franchise League and is on the executive of the James Connolly Labour College.

1921

Skinnider is involved in running a safe house, storing and transporting arms, training members in first aid, signalling and drilling. In October she becomes Director of Training for Cumann na mBan and a member of the Executive of Cumann na mBan. In October, her mother, Jane, drowns when the *SS Rowan*, en route from Dublin to Glasgow, sinks.

1922

Skinnider becomes Paymaster General for the anti-Treaty IRA as she takes an anti-Treaty stance. She is attached to the Quarter Master Generals (QMG) staff in the Four Courts until June. She is arrested on 26 December, charged with possession of a revolver, and imprisoned.

1923

Skinnider was imprisoned in Mountjoy and, later, in the North Dublin Union. Nóra O'Keeffe is arrested in February and imprisoned in Cork Jail and later in Kilmainham for her anti-Treaty activities.

1925

Skinnider remains active in politics and is a member of the Socialist Party of Ireland. She applies for a wound pension under the 1923 Army Pensions Act. She is refused.

1927

Skinnider and O'Keeffe are among the members of Cumann na mBan who attend Countess Markievicz's funeral. Skinnider gets a teaching post at the Sisters of Charity National School, King's Inn St., here she remains until her retirement. An avid trade unionist she becomes involved in the Irish National Teachers' Trade Union (INTO).

1930

Both Skinnider and O'Keeffe are among the women listed as involved in organisations considered dangerous by the Irish Free State's Criminal Investigation Department (CID).

1933

Skinnider is among the 37 women who attend the 1933 Cumann na mBan annual convention.

1938

Skinnider gets her military pension, 13 years after she first applied. She is awarded £80 per annum. Nóra O'Keeffe passes the Civil Service exam and become a clerical officer.

1940

Skinnider gives an interview to Raidió Éireann about her involvement in 1916 https://www.youtube.com/watch?v=2-zQbaGNAgU

1946

Skinnider is involved in organising the seven-month teachers' strike and serves on the strike committee. In July Skinnider becomes a founder member of the newly formed political party, Clann na Poblachta, led by the son of Maud Gonne McBride, Seán McBride.

1949

Skinnider becomes a Central Executive Committee (CEC) member of the INTO and will remain in that position until 1959. She represents the INTO on a committee (chaired by Judge P. J. Roe) formed by the Minister of Education to 'consider salaries and other grants including provision on retirement, to be an aid to teachers in national schools, and report theron'.

1950

Skinnider stands, unsuccessfully, for Clann na Poblachta in the local elections in Dublin in March. She is elected to the electoral panel of the party in June.

1953

Skinnider is elected to the Clann na Poblachta national executive in May. In May she is part of an INTO delegation who visit Seán Moylan, Minister for Education, to discuss the budget.

1955

Skinnider becomes Vice-President of the INTO and she is also elected to the Council of the Irish Professional and Services Association.

1956

Skinnider is elected President of the INTO on April 10. In July, she represents the union at the World Confederation of Organisations of the Teaching Profession in Manila, Philippines.

1959

ICTU establishes the Women's Advisory Committee, on which Margaret Skinnider and Eileen Liston represented the INTO. Skinnider is elected Chairman of the committee.

1961

Skinnider retires from teaching but remains an active trade union activist. She becomes a member of the Irish Congress of Trade Unions (ICTU).

1962

Nóra O'Keeffe dies in August. She is buried in her home county of Tipperary.

1963

The ICTU Women's Advisory Committee presses for women's issues in the trade union movement and pushes through a motion demanding equal pay.

1966

Skinnider does several interviews about the 1916 Rising as part of the 50th anniversary commemorations. She also gives a speech to the INTO about her experiences in 1916.

1971

Margaret Skinnider dies on October 10, 1971. Her funeral is in the Church of Our Lady of the Sorrows in Sallynoggin and is attended by representatives of the President, the Taoiseach, the INTO, old Cumann na mBan and other revolutionary comrades. She is buried in the Republican Plot in Glasnevin cemetery, beside her old revolutionary friend and comrade, Countess Constance Markievicz.

Introduction

When she applied for her military pension in October 1934, Helena Molony, who had been, like Margaret Skinnider, in the Irish Citizen Army (ICA) during 1916, was horrified that her service during the War of Independence was recorded by the Irish Free State as 'nil'. In a letter disputing this assertion, she stated that she wished to have the 'nil' erased from her record, not simply for her own sake, but because she was concerned 'with the recognition of women's services rendered to the Republic'.[1] In the same year she wrote to Seán Ó Faoláin, taking him to task for his critical biography of Countess Markievicz. O'Faoláin had depicted Markievicz not as an ideologically committed feminist, socialist and republican, but as a publicity hungry diva, who was 'caught up' in the excitement by the likes of 'Connolly, Larkin or some other men'.[2] Molony wrote that

> it's a curious thing that men seem to be unable to believe that any woman can embrace an ideal – accept it intellectually, feel it as a profound emotion, and then calmly decide to make a vocation of working for its realisation. They give themselves endless pains to prove that every serious thing a woman does (outside nursing babies or washing pots) is the result of being in love with some man or looking for excitement, or limelight, or indulging their vanity.[3]

Markievicz was, wrote Molony, 'working, as a man might have worked, for the freedom of Ireland'.[4] She was insistent that she and the other women in the ICA had done military service during the Easter Rising 1916. She challenged the gendered presumptions that the women were simply there to render First Aid, cook the food and look after the [male] soldiers. She noted that women were recruited into the ICA on the same terms as men and, like the men, appointed to the duties most suitable for them. These may have generally been 'dealing with Commissariat, Intelligence, First Aid and advanced Medical Aid', but, as she noted, 'they did other duties as well'.[5] In general, as she later recorded in a 1963 RTÉ Radio 1 interview, the women 'did whatever came to their hands to do, from day to day, and whatever they were capable of in aptitude or training'.[6] Like Skinnider and Markievicz, Molony had gone, armed, into the Easter Rising, and saw no issue with that. She was a combatant and would use whatever skills she had to fight for the freedom of Ireland. She and the other women who were members of the ICA promoted an 'idea of freedom [that] was the widest of its kind, the abolition of domination of nation over nation, class over class and sex over sex'.[7]

Margaret Skinnider would have found resonance in these ideas. On Easter Monday, 1916, she heard the Proclamation of the Republic read by Pearse outside the GPO, and it fitted with her ideal of a Republic where women would be on an 'equality with the men'.[8] As a young woman in Glasgow, she had been a militant suffragette fighting for the rights of women. She had also been concerned with the rights of workers, and those living in poverty and deprivation, and was associated with both the Catholic Socialist Party in Glasgow and the Socialist Party of Ireland. When she arrived in Dublin in December 1915, to visit Countess Markievicz, and was offered a tour around the city, she said what she really wanted to see was 'the poorest part of Dublin, the very poorest part'.[9] The Countess took her to Ashe Street, in the Liberties area of central Dublin. She was horrified at the living conditions of the people, living in houses which looked like 'cripples leaning on crutches'. These normally grand houses, which had been built for one family, now housed dozens in single rooms. But they had not been remodelled as such, so you would find 'in one room, perhaps a drawing room ... four families, each in its own corner'.[10] No money for food, heating or gas, as the head of each household generally earned less than 'four of five dollars a week ... on this amount if they wanted the luxury of even a small room to themselves they must pay a dollar'.[11] Furthermore, the Irish poor were always on the verge of starvation, despite the fact that 'Ireland could raise fruit and vegetables and grain for 20 million people'.[12] Poverty, hunger, low wages, and high infant mortality rates were the Irish 'grievances' which motivated Skinnider and so many like her.

Skinnider's book, *Doing My Bit for Ireland*, published in 1917 (The Century Co.), is one of the first female eye-witness accounts of the Rising. While written as a propaganda piece when she was on the republican women's tour in America post-Rising, it is also a chronology of her road to involvement in the 1916 Rising, through her involvement in suffrage and nationalist activism in Glasgow, and her contact with radical socialist, feminist and nationalist women and men in Dublin. She ends the book with a statement: 'Last November [1916] I paid a visit to Dublin. The bitterness had increased.'[13] This would not be the end of Skinnider's involvement in Irish politics and revolution. She would go on to play an active and important role in the War of Independence and Civil War as a senior member of Cumann na mBan. She would be a member of a cohort of left-leaning republicans who continued to influence politics in the Irish Free State, up to and including being a founder member of Clann na Poblachta. She would also be an important trade union activist through her membership of the Irish National Teachers' Organisation (INTO), of which she became President in 1956. Like her comrades and friends, Countess Markievicz, Nora

Connolly O'Brien, Hanna Sheehy Skeffington, Eithne Coyle, Sighle Humphreys, Kathleen Lynn, Madeleine ffrench-Mullen among others, her part in Irish history did not begin and end with Easter Week, 1916. Yet, like so many Irish revolutionary women, that would seem to be the case, particularly in the more traditional narratives of the fight for Irish Independence, the foundation of the Irish Free States and the history of the political, social and cultural development of that State into the twentieth century. Margaret Skinnider did not die until 1971; a militant suffragette of the first wave of feminism, she lived long enough to witness and have some impact on the beginning of second-wave feminism in Ireland. However, all too often she was remembered only as the 'sniper girl of Stephens Green', who was wounded in action in 1916, yet was denied a military pension as, according to the State she fought for, 'soldiers [were to be] generally understood in the masculine sense'.[14]

Generally, women who participated in the Easter Rising and the subsequent War of Independence were presumed to have been auxiliaries of the Irish Volunteers and the Irish Republican Army (IRA). Their histories were highly gendered, written through very specific categories of carer and nurturer. The presumption, as Molony and others insisted, that a woman could develop her own socialist or nationalist ideology was not often recognised or considered. Furthermore, the idea that a woman could be considered a combatant was extraordinary. When women such as Markievicz and Skinnider behaved contrary to gender expectations, their actions were perceived as unusual, as outliers, as performances which would not be expected or accepted in a peacetime society. The fact that she spent another 50 years as an activist is completely overlooked. Skinnider was driven, from an early age, by a commitment to the causes which Markievicz termed 'the three great movements of Ireland – the National movement, the Women's movement and the Industrial movement'.[15] From her late teens until she died, she devoted her energies to the freedom of Ireland, equality for women, and the rights of workers. She was prominent in almost all the organisations she joined, yet her place in history was, and continues in many ways to be, marginal. Indeed, one scholar wrote that 'Margaret Skinnider's bravery in the Uprising did not lead to a politically active career; after the turmoil was over she quietly settled down to be a school teacher'.[16] This close study of her life demonstrates that this analysis of Skinnider could not be further from the truth of a woman who never ceased campaigning for the rights and freedoms for the three causes to which she committed her life: Ireland, women and workers.

CHAPTER ONE

The Making of a Militant

On 28 May 1892, in Coatbridge, Scotland, a third daughter was born to an immigrant Irish father, James Skinnider, a stonemason, of Cornagilta, Tydavnet, County Monaghan, and his wife, Jane Doud, who was of Irish descent. Named Margaret Frances, she had two older sisters, Isabella and Mary, and three older brothers, Thomas, James and Joseph. A younger sister, Catherine Georgina, born in 1897, would complete the family. James Skinnider had left Monaghan in the 1870s. His family were tenant farmers on the Gertrude Rose Estate in Tydavnet. His father, Thomas, originally from Dungannon, had married Isabella Kelly. Thomas and Isabella Skinnider settled in Cornagilta, and James was born there in December 1846. The importance of the connection to Cornagilta is mentioned by Margaret in her 1917 memoir of the Easter Rising, *Doing My Bit for Ireland*. The Coatbridge Skinnider family often went on family visits and it was here Margaret learnt the histories of the seventeenth-century plantations of Ireland by Cromwellian settlers. On the way to her grandmother's family home, the Kelly farm at Cornagilta, seven miles outside Monaghan town, their 'jaunting car' would pass the 'fine places' of the 'stock' that came over with Cromwell, and were 'planted on Irish soil'.[1] It was then, she notes, that, as a young child she 'began to feel resentment'.

The Kelly family farm was on the estate of Miss Gertrude Rose, who inherited 3,942 acres from her uncle, James Rose, in

1841, and ran the estate until she died in 1907. Although there were some evictions from the Rose estate in the 1880s, and oral history does point to some harshness on the part of Miss Rose, it seems she was not wholly typical of the 'planter' type Skinnider mentioned.[2] Although often concerned with gaining as much income as possible from the estate, she was, in some ways, an improving landlady and in 1859 had a local school, along with a Principal Teachers' Residence, built for the local community. Francis Turner Palgrave, an art historian, poet and amateur architect, and friend of Miss Rose, who worked for the Education Department in Whitehall from 1849 to 1884, furnished the neo-Gothic design of the school. However, the area had plenty of tales of bad landlords to impact on an impressionable young mind. Margaret would have heard stories of Dacre Hamilton (died 1837) of nearby Cornacassa House, an agent for Lord Rossmore. Hamilton is reputed to have been the model for the land agent in William Carleton's *Valentine McClutchy: The Irish Agent*, published in 1846 (New York, D & J Sadlier). McClutchy is characterised as a land agent who manipulates his absentee landlord and his tenants for his own benefit. The local memory of the actual Dacre Hamilton was even worse, and Carleton, in his time in Monaghan, would have heard the stories of his cruelty and mistreatment of his tenants. While Hamilton is credited with improvements to Monaghan town, he is more often remembered as being unbendingly harsh to his tenants, and, as an Orangeman, a fierce opponent of the United Irishmen in the 1790s. Stories of Hamilton, a 'strange and vile character', held in 'loathing by the people of Monaghan', would have been still current when the Skinnider family came to Cornagilta for holidays.[3]

However influential as the stories of landlords and tenants in Monaghan were, it was in Coatbridge and later Glasgow that Margaret's education in Irish history evolved. Her father had left

Cornagilta in the 1870s and married Jane, her mother, in 1880, in Lanarkshire. Settling in Coatbridge, James Skinnider, who worked as a mason, found a large Irish emigrant population there. By the 1860s, 13 per cent of the population of nearby Glasgow was Irish born, and were, as Terence McBride notes, developing 'the nature of locally expressed Irish political identity'.[4] In nineteenth-century Glasgow, Irish involvement in popular associations evolved in tandem with politics in Ireland, with 'Trade Unionism, Ribbonism, O'Connell's Catholic Emancipation, and Repeal campaigns, Chartism and the temperance movement' all enjoying support. Coatbridge was a key stronghold of the Irish Home Rule movement, where major rallies were organised in the 1870s and 1880s, while the Irish National Land League (ILL) was organised there by 1881. While the growing Irish middle class were involved in Catholic Church-led educational and philanthropic work, there remained among working-class emigrants 'a secular-radical thread of activism [which] offered an alternative course for the Irish born'.[5] By the 1860s, the Irish Republican Brotherhood (IRB), an Irish militant, separatist secret society, was formed in both Coatbridge and Glasgow. Indeed, during Christmas 1865 there was a rumour, fuelled by the *Daily Mail*, that Fenians of Coatbridge were organising some kind of outbreak, either industrial sabotage or arms raids.[6] Within a short time, it is estimated, there were over 2,500 Fenians in Glasgow, with many thousands more in the more open National Brotherhood of Saint Patrick (which organised Saint Patrick's Day marches and other cultural activities), and other smaller Irish political and cultural organisations. Although the National Brotherhood was defunct by the time James Skinnider arrived in Coatbridge in the 1870s, there was a well organised Irish tradition of involvement in both the constitutional and the physical force traditions of Irish nationalist politics.

Integration of the Irish in Scotland was not easy, however, nor without violence. Sectarianism, anti-Irish sentiment among local workers, especially miners, dockers and shipyard workers who felt threatened by the influx of Irish during and after the Famine, and the ongoing class unrest, resulted in occasional outbreaks of violence against the Irish emigrants. In the 1870s and 1880s, the issues of land ownership and tenancy which hardened into the land war in Ireland, and the growing power of the Home Rule movement, also had an impact on the Coatbridge and Glasgow Irish. The creation of a mass movement among Irish tenants and among those who supported constitutional nationalism consolidated political opinion and solidarity, not just in Ireland but also among the emigrant Irish. In Glasgow, the *Glasgow Herald* of February 1882 noted that 'There can be little doubt that the Irishmen of Glasgow are today more united and more at one upon the political question concerning Ireland, than they have been for some years past.'[7] The land wars and the campaigns for Home Rule which also impacted on Glasgow, created a distrust of the Irish among the more loyal Scots, so it was an uneasy tension which sometimes erupted into sectarian, and anti-Irish, violence which the Skinnider family experienced in their early years in Scotland.

Through all these political developments, James Skinnider married and had to provide for his growing family. During their childhood, living among the Irish diaspora in Coatbridge, and later Glasgow, provided the Skinnider children with access to social, cultural and political organisations which kept them in contact with Ireland and Irish politics. While a British education was provided in their schooling, the cultural nationalist organisation, the Gaelic League, which was set up in Glasgow in 1895, provided a sense of connection to Ireland through its Irish language and history classes, as well as its social functions. One of the Irish visitors to Glasgow in 1902 was Patrick Pearse, who gave a well attended lecture on the Irish language in Scotland. He attached the revival of the language firmly to the national re-generation of Ireland and spoke of 'a battle to the death ... between the Irish mind and the English mind in Ireland'.[8] A book on Irish history lent to Margaret when she was twelve, and other influences, including becoming proficient in the Irish language through attendance at Irish language classes, helped develop in her the idea that the history of English oppression in Ireland should be told with tears, and with anger.[9]

By 1901 the Skinnider family had moved to Maryhill in Glasgow. James had been injured during his work as a mason and was, by 1911, a dealer in second-hand goods. The family were doing well enough financially to educate their children; by 1911, the older sisters Isabella (in a secondary school) and Mary (in a primary school) were both teachers, 18-year-old Margaret was a student teacher, while Catherine Georgina (called Georgie) was still in school. Margaret trained as a mathematics teacher for primary school. She graduated in June 1913 from the Notre Dame RC (Roman Catholic) Training College, Dowanhill, Glasgow. Her college report indicated that she was 'most capable student' who showed 'intelligent resourcefulness, sound independent judgment and high idealism'; qualities that would stand her in good stead as a teacher and as a revolutionary.[10] She had secured a job at St Peter's School, Partick, on the north side of Glasgow, by April 1913. She worked here until summer of 1914. She then worked in St Michael's Primary School in Parkhead, Glasgow until March 1915, and in St Agnes's Primary School in Lambhill, on the north side of the city, until April 1916.[11]

1912 seems to have been a pivotal year in the political development of Margaret Skinnider. As well as continuing her studies, she was now becoming more involved in suffrage activism in the city, and later acknowledged that she was known, by then, to the Glasgow police because of her militancy. The British militant suffrage organisation, the Women's Social and Political Union (WSPU), was set up in 1903, in London, by Emmeline Pankhurst and her daughter, Christabel. By 1906, the Scottish headquarters of the WSPU had been set up on Bath Street, in Glasgow. While most of the suffrage leadership was middle class, in Glasgow, as elsewhere, many working-class women were drawn into the movement, and from 1909 a wave of militant suffrage activity occurred in the city. Young Glaswegian working-class women such as Jessie Stephen, a domestic worker and founder, in 1911, of the Scottish Federation of Domestic Workers, became very involved in the militant campaigns of the WSPU. As with so many suffragettes in the city, Stephen, and later Skinnider, was a trade union activist and a socialist. She was involved in the Independent Labour Party (ILP) and chairperson of her local ILP branch in Maryhill in 1909. As Stephen later said of the Glasgow WSPU, 'We had a curious combination. You had very wealthy women, upper-class women and the ordinary working class, but we got on well together'.[12] In 1913 Stephen was the youngest member of the Glasgow delegation who joined the WSPU Suffrage Deputation of Working Women, who travelled to meet the British Prime Minister Lloyd George. This deputation was to show that the suffrage movement was not just a 'movement of rich women' and 'to shame the Labour party' for not representing women of the class they claimed to represent.[13]

Other WSPU members in Glasgow included the well-known working-class feminist and socialist, Helen Crawfurd. As Skinnider began her militant suffrage activism, Crawfurd, who would be influential in Skinnider's life, was one of the most notorious WSPU members in Glasgow. Crawfurd (née Jack) was born there in 1877 and married the Reverend Alexander Crawfurd in 1898. His ministry was among the poor of Glasgow, and on moving with him to his parish, she was shocked at the poverty, hunger and suffering of the working classes. At this time, she also developed an interest in the women's movement. In 1900 she joined the non-militant suffragists in the National Union of Women's Suffrage Societies (NUWSS). She regularly held meetings in her Glasgow home where the women would discuss issues such as 'sexual inequality and political and educational discrimination'.[14] In 1910, frustrated at the lack of progress on achieving the vote, she joined the WSPU and became a supporter of the militant tactics adopted by the organisation. She also educated herself on working women's conditions, reading 'Women and Economics' by Charlotte Perkins Gilman (Boston, 1898); 'Women and Labour' by Olive Schreiner (South Africa, 1911); and August Bebel's 'Socialism and Women' (New York, 1904).[15] In 1912 Crawfurd and eight other women from Glasgow took part in a mass raid by suffragettes in London: her job was to smash windows in the Department of Education. She believed that the militant tactics of the WSPU were necessary to force the Government to relent on female suffrage, reconciling it with her Christian faith by stating that, 'If Christ could be Militant, so could I.'[16] Because of this London action, Crawfurd received her first period of imprisonment; one month in Holloway Prison.

Militant suffrage activism continued in Glasgow during 1913 and 1914. In 1913, the suffragettes conducted what was termed a 'campaign of terror' across the city. Jessie Stephen began the militant actions for which she is best known, acid attacks on Glasgow letter boxes (envelopes with bottles of acid were posted to destroy the mail). Stephen later wrote that 'our militancy in Scotland ... took many forms such as the smashing of plate glass windows, going into art galleries and even attempts to burn down castles and stately homes'.[17] In March 1914, Mrs Pankhurst came to Glasgow as part of her Scottish tour. A meeting of the WSPU was held in St Andrew's Hall and it is likely that the militant suffragette Margaret Skinnider attended. As soon as Mrs Pankhurst appeared on the platform, the police emerged from hiding places and brutally broke up the meeting. Crawfurd vividly described the scene:

> the Hall which could hold about 3,000 was crowded, members of the Glasgow WSPU were stewarding the doors, the platform was beautifully decorated with flowers and banners, when Mrs Pankhurst stepped forward to address the crowd. Suddenly from hiding places around the Hall the police attacked, using their batons 'indiscriminately and women were bleeding and laid out'.[18]

The women fought back, and a shot was fired, Mrs Pankhurst was roughly handled and arrested, and the meeting broken up. Two days later, Crawfurd went out and smashed windows at an army recruiting office, was arrested, imprisoned for a month; and as she immediately went on hunger strike, she was released after eight days under the terms of the Cat and Mouse Act.[19]

Crawfurd's diaries reveal the exciting and difficult life of a militant suffragette in Glasgow, while also revealing the political ideologies of a committed feminist and socialist. They also show a connection with, and an understanding of, the Irish struggle for independence. 'Events in Ireland,' she wrote, 'disillusioned me as to the altruistic idealism of the ruling class'. That ruling class always changed the weapons of attack just when the workers seem near achieving their aim by 'constitutional means'. As with women's suffrage, constitutional campaigns proved futile, 'taken as evidence of weakness and incompetence to be flouted and exploited'.[20] Another entry in her diary demonstrates a closer connection to the Irish in Glasgow. In July 1914, two suffragettes were imprisoned at Perth Prison. As expected, they went on hunger strike, and the Glasgow WSPU gathered outside to protest and to support the imprisoned women. On 10 July 1914, there was a Royal Visit of George V and Queen Mary to Glasgow, and Crawfurd wanted to protest at that. Her place was taken on the picket line at Perth Prison by 'Margaret Skinnider, an Irishwoman'. Crawfurd wrote that Skinnider offered to 'take my place to enable me to go see the procession. Margaret had no time for Kings and Queens'.[21] Crawfurd protested the Royal Visit, where she was re-arrested, taken back by police to Perth Prison, and held there. She immediately went on hunger strike and was released after five days.

This brief reference to the 'Irishwoman' places Skinnider at the centre of militant suffrage action in Glasgow. By then, she was 22 years old and had been a teacher in St Michael's Primary School for over a year. It is evident from the diary entry that Crawfurd knew Skinnider well enough to know of her Irish background. This would indicate that Skinnider was a known participant in the militant suffrage activities in Glasgow. She had not herself been arrested but was, as she later admitted, known to the Glasgow police for her militancy. Suffrage militancy escalated in Glasgow into the summer months of 1914. Bomb attacks had been made on Kibble Palace Glasshouse at the Botanic Gardens in January 1914, and Crawfurd was arrested for this event. In April, three small bombs went off at Belmont Church on Great George Street in the west of the city. Not long after, suffragettes made an unsuccessful attempt, with two quite powerful bombs whose fuse failed, to blow up the aqueduct bringing the city's clean water supply from Loch Katrine.

On 4 August 1914, however, war broke out. The NUWSS suspended all political activity and, as the Government announced it was releasing all suffragettes from prison, the WSPU agreed to suspend all its activities and help the war effort. In common with fellow radical suffragettes, Sylvia Pankhurst, Charlotte Despard,

Emmeline Pethick-Lawrence and Olive Schreiner, Crawfurd disagreed with this course of action. In March 1915, she formed a branch of the United Suffragists in Glasgow, and among its members were many women who had been members of the WSPU. The United Suffragists had been set up in February 1914, composed of suffragettes and male allies, who disapproved of the arson campaigns of the WSPU and who were disillusioned by the lack of success of the moderate, constitutional suffragists of NUWSS. In common with most United Suffragists, the Glasgow members disagreed with the suspension of suffrage activism in 1914 and wished to continue to campaign for women's suffrage during the war. The Glasgow United Suffragists held a meeting in the city on 28 October 1915, to discuss the fact that 'except for the activities of the Freedom League, the question of women's suffrage has been allowed to lapse altogether in Glasgow since the outbreak of war'.[22] Mrs Pethick-Lawrence was coming 'to stir them up' and among the women who attended were 'Mrs Crawfurd ... Miss Swan, Miss Barrowman, Miss Corrigan and Miss Skinnider'.[23] Here again is evidence of the involvement of Skinnider with the Glasgow suffragettes.

By this time, however, Skinnider had other political interests. While many of the women in the United Suffragists were also members of organisations such as the Women's International League for Peace and Freedom, or the Glasgow Women's Housing Association,[24] Skinnider was now more active in Irish organisations. In 1909, Countess Markievicz and Bulmer Hobson had launched Na Fianna Éireann, an Irish Boy Scouts' movement, in Dublin. It was set up 'in order to counteract the influence in Ireland of the pro-British Boy Scouts' movement'.[25] By 1910, a sluagh, or branch, of Na Fianna was formed in Glasgow by Joe Robinson, who was appointed Officer Commanding (O/C) of the branch. Early members of the Glasgow Sluagh were Joe's brother, Séumas

Robinson, Eamonn Mooney and Seamus Reader, all of whom Skinnider knew.[26] She seems to have been associated with the Glasgow Fianna Sluagh from the beginning and, by 1913, she 'trained and drilled' the boys with Seamus Reader.[27] In 1913, a branch of the militant nationalist organisation, the Irish Volunteers, was set up in in the city, and Skinnider became associated with that. By mid-1915, a branch of the women's militant nationalist organisation, Cumann na mBan, was also organised there. This she also joined, later becoming Captain of the branch. This Anne Devlin Branch was to be her home in Cumann na mBan until she moved permanently to Ireland in March 1919. Between 1912 and 1916 Skinnider's militancy moved between militant suffrage activism and militant nationalism, and both ideologies were to inform her politics for the rest of her life.

When war broke out in 1914, she decided to join one of the 'rifle practice clubs which the British organised so that women could help in defense of Empire'.[28] However, in becoming an expert shot, she intended to use her skills not in 'defense of Empire', rather she awaited the opportunity to fight to 'defend my own country [Ireland]'.[29] By 1914, the political situation in Ireland was quite tense. The 3rd Home Rule bill, to establish an Irish Parliament in Dublin to deal with Irish affairs, had passed in 1912, and was due to come into effect in 1914. This met with huge opposition from Unionists in Ireland, particularly among the majority Unionist population in Ulster. In September 1912, over 500,000 Ulster Unionists signed the Solemn League and Covenant, or 'Ulster Covenant', in protest against the Home Rule bill, and pledging to block any attempts to implement Home Rule. In order to do this, the Ulster Volunteer Force (UVF) was formed in January 1913 and, by March 1914, had armed themselves with 20,000 German rifles with 3,000,000 rounds of ammunition, smuggled in during the Larne gunrunning. To counteract this armed Unionist militia, the

Irish Volunteers, who supported the introduction of Home Rule, were established in November 1913 in Dublin. The Irish Volunteers also sought to arm themselves, and in July 1914 over 900 rifles were offloaded at Howth, outside Dublin.

In Scotland, the Irish Volunteer branches, along with the secretive, militant, Fenian organisation, the IRB, aided by Na Fianna and Cumann na mBan, sought to do their bit in arming the Irish Volunteers in Ireland. The Fenians had been active in Scotland and Glasgow since the 1860s, and the IRB still had a strong presence there. One of the men known to Skinnider, Daniel Branniff, from Dromara, County Down, had been in the Glasgow IRB since 1907 and served, between 1912 and 1914, as representative for Scotland on the Supreme Council of the IRB. Brothers Joe and Séumas Robinson were also in the IRB, as was Seamus Reader. The connections between Ireland and Glasgow were solid, with regular visits from activists, both socialist and nationalist, such as Patrick Pearse, James Connolly, and Liam Mellows, and from nationalist feminists such as Countess Markievicz, Nora Connolly and Maud Gonne MacBride. Suffragettes Charlotte Despard and Hanna Sheehy Skeffington also visited and spoke on platforms with the Scottish suffrage activists. A section of the unpublished memoirs of Helen Crawfurd deals with Ireland, and reveals the close connections between socialist, feminist and nationalist activists in Ireland and Scotland. As a militant suffragette, she felt she had a keen appreciation of the situation in which the Irish people found themselves from 1914, especially as the introduction of Home Rule was suspended on the outbreak of war. As she wrote, 'after years of constitutional work for Home Rule, they [the Irish] were to be flouted and defied by the forces of reaction'.[30] Speaking often on platforms in Belfast and Dublin for the ILP, she was very aware of the work of James Connolly and Jim Larkin for the rights of workers. She remembered Larkin coming to Scotland in 1913 to plead for support for the striking Dublin workers during the Lockout, and Connolly, she said, knew the value of the work of women in a revolutionary struggle.[31]

Scotland was a vital link in the planning, arming and organising of militant Irish nationalism. With constant travel back and forth, and strong political connections with the large Irish emigrant population, the Glasgow-Belfast-Dublin triangle was 'very active in the smuggling of weapons and explosives and the arrival of Scottish republicans' from 1915 onwards.[32] While arms had been smuggled in at Howth in 1914, the Irish Volunteers continued to be desperately short of rifles, ammunition, bomb-making equipment, and explosives. In the Glasgow shipyards, however, munitions and explosives were to be found in abundance. Irish Volunteer, Séumas Robinson, detailed the activities of Na Fianna and the Volunteers in Glasgow during this time:

> Na Fianna … were very active in raiding munitions factories and mines for explosives … This activity increased as 1916 approached. The raids had become almost 'barefaced' – they had got away with so much for so long without detection. At last a sort of grand finalé was planned and carried out at Addington [shipyards], I think it was, when a big haul of explosives was captured.[33]

As a trusted militant and member of Cumann na mBan Margaret Skinnider was one of the people who participated in the raids on shipyards, along with Na Fianna boys (whom she had been training and drilling) and members of the Irish Volunteers. She, and other members of the Anne Devlin Branch of Cumann na mBan, were involved in 'raids at shipyards and mining facilities in the West of Scotland … for arms, explosives and ammunition'.[34] The women were important to ruses used to deflect suspicion:

the Cumann na mBan were brought in with the Volunteers for this raid. These included Una McKeown, Margaret Skinnider, Molly Maguire. Volunteers were Joe Robinson, Hagerty, Séamus McGallogly. These were supposed to be boy and girl friends and went out together so as not to arouse suspicion.[35]

Skinnider, in a 1917 letter, claimed that 'in one night we took 500lbs of explosives'.[36] More important than participation in the raids, however, was the use of the militant Cumann na mBan women to hide and transport any explosives and munitions stolen in these raids back to Ireland. British intelligence was aware of the activities of the IRB and the Volunteers in Britain, and there were spies constantly watching known Irish subversives; for instance, Joe Robinson and Seamus Reader were arrested in January 1916. The routes between Glasgow, Belfast and Dublin were also watched by police, and it was difficult and dangerous to smuggle weapons and explosives into Ireland. However, a woman travelling on these routes was regarded with less suspicion and so the Cumann na mBan women were often used to transport arms, explosives and messages from Scotland to Ireland. Some of this bomb-making material also went to the ICA; Scotland was one of the few places outside of Ireland where there was support for the ICA, especially among socialist activists on the Clydeside.

In December 1915, Margaret Skinnider sailed to Dublin at the invitation of that 'most patriotic and revolutionary of women in all Ireland', Countess Markievicz.[37] Not one to waste an opportunity she travelled across the Irish Sea with detonators and bomb wires concealed on her person. She was not the only Anne Devlin Branch member who did this dangerous work, however. A Miss O'Neill also transported explosives from time to time, as did Lizzie Morrin, a dressmaker, who had made clothing with 'hidden pockets for unobtrusive smuggling of ammunition'.[38] The danger of the work was vividly recalled by Skinnider. On the rough December crossing, she was aware that pressure could set off the equipment she was carrying:

> In my hat I was carrying ... detonators for bombs, and the wires were wrapped around under my coat. That was why I had not wanted to go to a stateroom where I might run into a hot water pipe or an electric wire what would set them off. But pressure, they told me when I reached Dublin, is just as dangerous, and my head had been resting heavily on them all night![39]

As she travelled to Dublin that December 1915, Skinnider already had more than four years' experience of militant activism behind her. A seasoned militant suffragette and advanced militant nationalist, she was already committed to the three causes which would inform her politics for the rest of her life – the cause of women, the cause of workers and the cause of Ireland. In Dublin she would meet many of the people she knew already, including James Connolly, through her friend and his daughter, Nora Connolly (whom she got to know in Glasgow on one of Nora's regular visits there), and Countess Markievicz whom she knew of and admired by reputation. Skinnider's journey to radical, militant feminism and advanced nationalism had occurred among the large Irish populations in Coatbridge and Glasgow, so her visit to Dublin in December 1915 would continue her life on a path on which she had already begun. 'Scotland was,' she wrote, her home, but from now on, Ireland, was 'my country'.[40]

CHAPTER TWO

The 1916 Rebel

Skinnider devotes more than 30 pages of her 1917 memoir, *Doing My Bit for Ireland*, detailing her 1915 visit to Dublin. This indicates the importance of that visit, and of how she came to be accepted as a trusted insider by those she admired most, Connolly and Markievicz.[1] In 1917, in New York, writing her memoir, she wrote that 'it was hard ... to think of that hospitable house in Leinster Road with all the life gone out of it and its Mistress in an English prison.'[2] This was Surrey House, the home of Countess Markievicz between 1912 and 1916. Here Skinnider was to meet many of the men and women she would fight beside in 1916, as Markievicz kept an open house which was visited by 'everyone ... who was interested in plays, painting, the Gaelic Language, suffrage, labour, or Irish Nationalism'.[3] She wrote with pride of her revelation to Markievicz that she could pass as a boy, 'even when it came to wrestling or whistling'.[4] Her tactics of 'gender subversion', her skill in fading in and out of the male ranks without detection ... earned the much desired attention of Markiewicz'.[5] So proud was she of her ability to pass as male that she included a photograph of herself dressed as a member of Na Fianna, 'in boys drag, with cigarette definitely slung from her lips' in her 1917 book.[6] Interestingly, this is a doctored version of the original 1915 photograph. In the original, the gender transgression is even more obvious, with Skinnider in a Fianna boys costume, a cigarette

slung from her lips, and two young women, on either side, linking
arms with her; it is, for all the world, the photo of a young man
escorting two young ladies out for a walk. Who made the editorial
decision, and why, to include the doctored version in the 1917 book
is unknown. Some women, especially those in the ICA, dressed
like their male comrades. The image of a rebel woman dressing in
male drag for the specific purposes of war was more acceptable, in
relative terms, for public consumption, than the image of a woman
in male drag enjoying the company of other women.

While in Dublin Skinnider participated in various activities
with Na Fianna and got to know many of the advanced nationalists
active there. She went on route marches with the boys, while
dressed and passing as one of them, singing anti-recruitment
songs as they marched through the Dublin streets. Markievicz
lived near Portobello Barracks and Beggars' Bush, two of several
large military barracks housing British Army regiments, situated
in and around Dublin. Markievicz asked her if she 'thought [she]
could make a plan of the latter [Beggars' Bush] from observation
that would be of use if at any time it was decided to dynamite
them'.[7] With her mathematical training, Skinnider was able to
study the Barracks buildings and defensive walls, both from maps
and by sight, and produced detailed sketches and a plan of how to
effectively blow it up. Walking the streets, this time as a woman, she
was able to pass unnoticed. Indeed, while she was very proud to
pass as a boy, she now quite consciously used her femininity to get
details of the barracks:

> When I reached the spot where I thought that the [powder] magazine
> ought to be, I took my handkerchief and let it blow – accidentally of
> course – over this outer wall. A [male] passer-by gallantly offered to
> get it for me, Being a woman and naturally curious, I found it necessary
> to pull myself up on tiptoe to watch him as he climbed over the wall.[8]

While strolling around Beggars' Bush, she was able to get details of the buildings which allowed her to complete her sketch and the plans to dynamite the barracks. Markievicz showed these to James Connolly, leader of the Irish Citizen Army (ICA), the small but militant workers militia set up during the 1913 Lockout. The ICA allowed women to join on an equal basis as men, and many of the left-leaning, socialist women, such as Markievicz, Dr Kathleen Lynn, Madeleine ffrench-Mullen, Helena Molony, as well as working-class women, all members of the Irish Women's Workers' Union (IWWU), such as Rosie Hackett, Brigid Davis and Jennie Shanahan, were members. Connolly was, it seems, impressed by Skinnider's plans, and, she noted, 'from that day [she] was taken into the confidence of the movement for making Ireland a Republic'.[9]

While she was in Dublin she also took part in raids on ships moored on the River Liffey, seeking, as she had in the Admiralty shipyards in Glasgow, to steal explosives. Much of the stolen material was hidden in Surrey House. 'Bombs and rifles were hidden in absurd places for she [Markievicz] had the skill to do it and escape detection'.[10] As a French journalist who came to visit Markievicz shorty before the Rising noted, 'the salon of the Countess Markievicz is not a salon … it is a military headquarters.'[11] Skinnider and Markievicz also made expeditions up the Dublin mountains, with Na Fianna boys, where they tested dynamite. She also got to know many of the leaders of advanced nationalism in Dublin. These included Proclamation signatory and IRB man, Thomas McDonagh, who gave her a gift of a revolver, which she would use during the Rising. Skinnider had now firmly decided her place was in Ireland for the coming insurrection. It would seem that she had been entrusted with some details of the plan to rise at Easter. She returned to Glasgow, and her teaching post, now in St Agnes' Primary School, in January 1916, and promised to be back in Dublin before Easter. She told her mother of the plans for the

Rising. Her mother was not convinced that any Irish rising could succeed but Skinnider was moved by the spirit of unity and revolution she found in Dublin: 'dock workers, schoolteachers, poets and bartenders. They were all working together ... I believed they would stand and fight together. And I was right.'[12]

On Holy Thursday, 20 April 1916, Skinnider returned to Dublin. She joined with the ICA who were headquartered at Liberty Hall. Markievicz was a senior member of the ICA, and Nora Connolly, was also involved. She was immediately put to work, initially helping the women in Liberty Hall make cartridges, but was soon sent by James Connolly with a dispatch to his home in Belfast, when she again met Nora Connolly. She had arrived in Dublin just as plans for the Rising were coming undone in the south west of the country, in County Kerry. A German ship, *The Aud*, was expected in Tralee Bay, on Easter Sunday, with a large shipment of arms and ammunition for the Irish Volunteers. The arms were to be distributed to Volunteer branches in the west and south of the country, enabling them to take part in the armed uprising. However, *The Aud* arrived into Tralee Bay on Holy Thursday, with no one expecting it or there to meet it. This was just one of several calamities which happened in Kerry, on 20 and 21 April, which would directly impact on the plans for the Rising. On Good Friday, Sir Roger Casement, who had negotiated the arms delivery from Germany, arrived at Banna Strand in the north of the county and was soon arrested. *The Aud* was eventually discovered by the British and taken under arms to Cork Harbour. By then, 'word of the unfolding tragedy and chaos' had reached Eoin MacNeill, Chief of Staff of the Irish Volunteers. He issued a countermand calling off the Rising and followed it up with an advertisement to that effect in the *Sunday Independent* of 23 April.[13]

Skinnider described the shock felt by those in Dublin who were preparing for the Rising when they heard of MacNeill's countermand. Coming out of Mass on Easter Sunday morning, she saw

the headline, 'No Volunteer Manoeuvres Today' on placards
everywhere. This was, she said:

> astounding! The manoeuvres were to be the beginning of the
> Revolution. Today they were not to be the usual, simple drill, but a real
> beginning of military action. All over Ireland the Volunteers were
> expected to mobilise and stay mobilised until the blow was struck –
> until, perhaps, victory had been won.[14]

The MacNeill countermand, although it had the effect of stopping
countrywide uprisings, was itself quickly countermanded. The
leaders in the ICA, the Supreme Council of the IRB, and the Irish
Volunteers, altered the plan, choosing now to commence the
Rising on Easter Monday, April 24, instead. However, confusion
about the orders from MacNeill and the subsequent decision to go
ahead with the Rising on Easter Monday meant that fewer than
1,500 men and about 300 women participated in the Rising, and
resulted in the Rising being mainly confined to Dublin.[15] Among
the 300 women who did participate was Margaret Skinnider, and
she did so with the ICA, under the command of Michael Mallin
and his second in command, Countess Markievicz.

The small ICA, ideologically influenced by its leader – socialist
and trade union activist – James Connolly, had proven more
attractive to many of the radical feminists, female nationalists and
women trade union members, than Cumann na mBan. Connolly,
described by Francis Sheehy Skeffington, editor of the suffrage
newspaper, *The Irish Citizen*, as 'the soundest and most thorough-
going feminist among all the Irish labour men', had formed
friendships and alliances with many of the militant suffrage,
separatist and labour women.[16] These more radical women did not
approve of the fact that at its foundation in 1914, Cumann na
mBan positioned itself as an auxiliary to the men in the Irish
Volunteers. That many of the left-leaning, middle-class women

chose to join the ICA rather than Cumann na mBan reflects their political engagement in suffrage activism, in radical social activism through trade union politics, and in advanced nationalism. Working-class female members of the ICA had been politicised through membership of the women's trade union, the IWWU, established in 1911, and through their involvement in the 1913 Lockout. Although the ICA had a 'women's section', many of the female members felt that there was an egalitarian aspect in the ICA. Markievicz wrote that women were:

> on absolutely the same footing as the men. They took part in all the marches, even in the manoeuvres that lasted all night. Connolly made it quite clear to us that unless we women took our share of the drudgery in training and preparing, we would not be allowed take any share in the fight.[17]

As part of their training, the ICA women drilled, trained with arms, marched, and received First Aid instruction from Dr Kathleen Lynn. Helena Molony, who had been involved in the militant, separatist, feminist group, Inghinidhe na hÉireann, from 1900, and was editor of their newspaper, *Bean na hÉireann*, was also a member of the ICA. In the week prior to the Rising she noted that the members were on high alert:

> the Rising might take place any day as far as I was concerned. Our little group of women were on the alert practically the whole time. There were eight girls in the work-room over the shop. Jinny Shanahan and two others around the shop. Rosie Hackett travelled for collections and I was checking up accounts, etc. There would be no need to tell us to be there.[18]

Many of the women were sleeping in Liberty Hall in the fortnight preceding the Rising. On Easter Sunday, the ICA, among them

Skinnider, went on a route march, and 'the bugler sounded his bugle at each of the places that were taken in the Rising'.[19] That evening, most were ordered to stay in Liberty Hall until further notice and, as Rosie Hackett later wrote, 'Connolly told us we would have to buck up and get ready, that the day was coming.'[20]

When the Rising began on Easter Monday 1916, it was a small, chaotic affair confined mainly to Dublin. All members of the ICA were required to be at Liberty Hall at midday to receive their orders. Some were to go with Seán Connolly to Dublin Castle, some to St Stephen's Green with Michael Mallin and Countess Markievicz, and others to the GPO on O'Connell Street with Connolly. In Skinnider's case, as a dispatch rider and scout, she was sent on her bicycle to 'scout about the city and report if troops from any of the barracks were stirring'.[21] When she returned with her report, she was sent out again by Michael Mallin to scout St. Stephen's Green. If there was no unusual police or military activity to report, she was to remain there until joined by Mallin and his contingent. Just before noon she set off to St. Stephen's Green. Nothing unusual was happening there, so she waited for the 'great moment' when, between the branches of trees, she caught sight of 'men in dark green uniforms coming along in twos and threes to take up their positions in and about the Green and at the corners of streets leading into it'.[22] There were far fewer men and women than had been expected, because of the confusion over the countermand, but for Skinnider and all the insurgents in Dublin that morning, 'the revolution had begun!'.[23]

As Mallin's small garrison set about entrenching themselves in the Green, it was soon obvious that it would be a very difficult position to defend.[24] However, as it was a quiet Bank Holiday Monday, the response of the police and military was slow, giving the insurgents time to settle in. The city's inhabitants had become used to militant organisations going on their regular route marches, and the sight of uniformed men and women in the Green was initially more an annoyance than a threat. In fact, the tall figure of Markievicz, in her self-designed uniform of 'an Irish Citizen Army tunic, a pair of riding breeches and puttees and a lady's hat with an ostrich feather' was inclined to cause comment and amusement rather than fear.[25] However, the insurgents were there with deadly intent this time. This soon became obvious when they commandeered carriages and vehicles to blockade the Green. Markievicz oversaw the trench digging in the Green, while Mallin organised the blockades. In the Green, the ICA and Cumann na mBan women set up First Aid stations. Almost immediately Skinnider was sent on the first of several dispatch missions from Mallin to Connolly, who was stationed in the General Headquarters (GHQ) of the insurgents, the GPO on O'Connell St.

On the first dispatch mission, she arrived in time to hear Pearse read the Proclamation of the Republic 'at the foot of Nelson's Pillar'.[26] The Proclamation, with its inclusion of equality for women, was to be a touchstone for Skinnider and many of the other revolutionary women for the rest of their lives. For many of the revolutionary women this was the Ireland they committed their lives to, a Republic in which they would be full and equal citizens. They were now – as promised in the Proclamation – she would later insist to Mallin, 'on an equality with men'.[27] Throughout the day Skinnider cycled back and forth with various dispatches and on various scouting missions. As the day went on the danger for the dispatch carriers, mostly women, increased. The Dublin Metropolitan Police (DMP) and some contingents of the British Army were finally beginning to respond to the presence of armed insurgents holed up in many buildings throughout the city. However, Skinnider felt relatively safe that first day. She would have looked simply a young woman innocently cycling her bicycle through the city: why would she be stopped and questioned? And she wasn't.

As night fell of the first day of the Rising she and the rest of the garrison settled down in the Green. The women bedded down as best they could in the summer house, and although it was a cold, damp night, Skinnider 'slept at once and slept heavily'.[28] That sleep was not to last long, however. The British forces had finally managed to get men and arms into several of the tall Georgian houses around the Green, including the Shelbourne Hotel. At 4 am they began firing on the insurgents camped in the Green. Very quickly it was obvious that the situation there was untenable, and that the garrison needed to retreat to one of the large buildings they had earlier secured, the Royal College of Surgeons (RCSI), on the west side of the Green. Even the women in the Red Cross shelter were not safe. With little option left, Mallin ordered a general evacuation from the Green to the RCSI and sent Skinnider with a dispatch to the GHQ at the GPO to inform Connolly and Pearse of this move. On that second day of the Rising, cycling through the city was much more dangerous. British troops were, by now, stationed in many places, particularly around the city centre through which she had to pass. On a dispatch to Leeson Street to tell the 16 men guarding the Leeson Street Bridge to come the RCSI, Skinnider had her first taste 'of the risks of street fighting'.[29] When she cycled her bicycle towards Leeson Street:

> soldiers on top of the Hotel Shelbourne aimed their machine-gun directly at me. Bullets struck the wooden rim of my bicycle wheels, puncturing it; others rattled on the metal rim or among the spokes. I knew one might strike me at any moment, so I rode as fast as I could. My speed saved my life, and I was soon out of range around a corner.[30]

On retuning she joined the garrison in the RCSI. They were to remain there for the rest of the week. While the RCSI offered the protection of thick walls – 'the British may as well have been firing "dried peas" at the walls for all the damage they did' – the garrison was increasingly pinned down in the building.[31] Despite this, they quickly settled in. Snipers were positioned on the roof, sleeping and provision quarters were set up. The women set up a First Aid station in a secluded area in the main College Lecture Hall, and the building was searched for arms. A tricolour, which Skinnider had brought back from the GPO, was hoisted over the building.

By Wednesday, there was little dispatch carrying for the women to do, as, although the garrison were relatively safe in the RCSI, they could not move about without coming under sustained fire. Skinnider's scouting abilities were also under utilised and she now wished to put her shooting skills to use. She had a fine uniform to change into; it was of green moleskin, which Markievicz had given her, and consisted of 'knee breeches, belted coat and puttees'.[32] She took off her women's clothes which she had worn while dispatch carrying and slipped into her moleskin uniform, climbed up on to the roof and 'was assigned a loophole through which to shoot'.[33] Her constant changing of clothes for the different roles she played in the Rising indicates an understanding of the gendered roles expected of men and women. Women could be part of the Rising, but to be soldiers they had to be in male attire. When she was sent to deliver dispatches, she pulled on her 'grey dress and hat', and as soon as she returned, she 'slipped back into my uniform and joined the firing squad'.[34] Her skills, honed at the women's rifle club in Glasgow, served her well, and 'more than once I saw the man I aimed at fall'.[35] At times, while out scouting, she had come upon British soldiers, but did not engage them militarily as 'I was not in uniform … and had had orders not to shoot except thus clothed and so a member of the Republican

Army'.[36] As a scout and a dispatch carrier, her female dress allowed her pass under the radar, as women were not expected to be combatants. She was evidently conscious that being a soldier was only possible when clothed in male attire. This tension between Skinnider's performance of femininity (which gave her such success as a scout) and her determination to be a soldier (in full uniform) inflects much of her depiction of the Rising in her memoir.

She also understood the frustration felt by Mallin and Markeivicz as they continued to be pinned down in the RCSI. Mallin sent some men to tunnel through neighbouring houses, without much success. Skinnider then came to him with a proposal. She wanted to lead a bomb attack on the Shelbourne Hotel where some of the machine guns, which constantly raked the College, were stationed. She proposed that she 'go out with one man and try to throw a bomb attached to an eight-second fuse through the hotel window'.[37] Mallin baulked at the idea of allowing a woman to go into such danger but she forcefully reminded him that:

> we [women] had the same right to risk our lives as the men; that in the Constitution [Proclamation] of the Irish Republic, women were on an equality with men. For the first time in history, indeed, a constitution had been written that incorporated the principle of equal suffrage.[38]

While the plan to bomb the Shelbourne was not acted on, she did persuade Mallin to let her lead a small group from the College, to take out sniper positions on University Church and the Russell Hotel near Harcourt Street, which were also pinning the RCSI garrison down. The plan was to set nearby buildings on fire and hope that the resulting smoke would impede any snipers' line of fire. Mallin reluctantly agreed, so early on Thursday morning, about 2 am, Skinnider, with a small group, advanced slowly towards

Harcourt St and University Church. As they reached Harcourt Street, ICA man William Partridge used the butt of his rifle to break in a door which, unfortunately, set his rifle off. The flash gave away their position: they were fired on, 'with the result that Freddie Ryan was killed, and I was wounded. I got three wounds'.[39]

Partridge and the others managed to get the badly wounded Skinnider back to the RCSI. She had two gunshots to the right shoulder, and one wound a quarter inch from her spine.[40] The garrison at the College feared she was dying, and the women in charge of First Aid, under the direction of Madeleine ffrench-Mullen, had to operate to save her life. They probed the wounds without anaesthetic to remove the bullets. Frank Robbins described her condition, which he observed when he was brought in to help turn her:

> we learned from Miss French-Mullen [sic] that our job was to transfer the wounded Miss Skinnider from one bed to another in such a manner to avoid any further loss of blood or causing her any more pain … throughout the transfer Miss Skinnider was deeply unconscious. She lost a great deal of blood and appeared to us to be on the verge of death.[41]

That she survived was a testament to the excellent First Aid training that the ICA and Cumann na mBan women had received. She was no longer able to play an active part in the Rising, but she remained in the RCSI until the surrender on Sunday. As the British authorities tightened their grip on the city, the garrison in the College was left feeling increasingly isolated.

On Saturday morning 'a dismaying rumour' circulated that the garrison in the GPO had surrendered.[42] ICA member, Rosie Hackett, recalled seeing 'Madame [Markievicz] one time, sitting on the stairs, with her head in her hands', and Mallin looking 'pale ... drawn and haggard', shaking hands with everybody.[43] On Sunday morning, a 'dispatch girl, white and scared' because she had been escorted to 'our fort by British soldiers' came to inform them that a general surrender had been called.[44] Mallin and Markievicz convinced the garrison that as soldiers their duty was to follow orders and surrender. After they surrendered most of the garrison were arrested and marched off to Richmond Barracks. Skinnider, wounded but conscious, was not with them. As she was being carried by stretcher to the waiting ambulance to be transported across the Green to nearby St. Vincent's Hospital, the Countess slipped her will inside the lining of Skinnider's coat. It was the end of the Rising for the insurgents and for Skinnider. She did not yet know of the extent of the damage done to the city by the fighting, or of the fate of her friends and comrades. As she lay in hospital in the following days and week, dozens of her female comrades were held in Richmond Barracks, Mountjoy and Kilmainham Gaol. In Kilmainham Gaol they heard the dawn gunshots which took the lives of 15 men, the signatories of the Proclamation and other leaders, including the Commandant of the RCSI garrison, Michael Mallin, and her friend Nora Connolly's father, James, head of the ICA. Her beloved comrade, Countess Markievicz, was also court martialled and sentenced to death but this was commuted to life imprisonment because of her gender. Hundreds of men were rounded up and transported to prison camps in England and Wales, and the organisations which had planned and carried out the Rising were depleted and in disarray. The Ireland that Skinnider had known and the life that she had led would be very different once she recovered and was released from hospital.

CHAPTER THREE

'Doing Her Bit'
Politics and Propaganda

The weeks Skinnider spent in St Vincent's Hospital after the surrender were, she wrote, the 'blackest of my life'.[1] She was seriously ill: her wounds were open and needed constant dressing and she had contracted pneumonia. As she lay there, unable to move, news of the executions of the leaders of 1916 drifted into the hospital. Nora Connolly, who had visited her father in Dublin Castle the night before his execution, came to visit her. She told Skinnider of James Connolly's last hours. He had, she said, 'anxiously enquired after Margaret', and 'praised her bravery' during Easter Week.[2] Although her sister came from Glasgow to be with her, Skinnider was anxious to get out and home to Scotland, especially after a policeman arrived in St Vincent's and insisted she be discharged into his custody. She was taken to the Bridewell Police Station for questioning. It was obvious, however, that she was still very ill, so she was released back to the hospital. There she remained another two weeks, before leaving of her own accord. Travelling through the streets of Dublin, she was horrified at the destruction: 'Dublin was scarred and, it seemed to me, very sick.'[3] Liberty Hall was a shell, many buildings around O'Connell Street were levelled, but she was happy to see that the GPO, although a blackened shell, was still standing, as 'that great building stood there like a monument to Easter Week'.[4] Martial law had been declared, so she had to apply to Dublin Castle for a special permit to travel home. Her Scottish accent and the fact that she looked 'more like a teacher of mathematics, which indeed I am, than like an Irish rebel, of which I am more proud', meant she received her permit without any suspicion that she had been a participant in Easter Week.[5]

Back in Scotland, she recuperated. She soon had an offer of a teaching job the following September in St John's School, but she only stayed there for two months. She had not given up her republican activities. She was proud to report that only a few 'Irish revolutionaries' were held in Scotch prisons, as there was 'too much sympathy ... for them [from] the Irish in Glasgow and from [the] Scotch suffragettes'.[6] While in Scotland she continued her revolutionary activism as much as she could; she travelled to visit the Irish revolutionaries being held in Reading Jail, where she found them in good spirits. She also re-joined the nationalist and socialist organisations she had previously been a member of and met with old comrades. After her RCSI garrison comrade, ICA man Frank Robbins, was released from prison camp, he went to Glasgow and met her at a Catholic Socialist Party meeting.[7] She asked Robbins to take 'messages' to her brother Thomas who was living in New York; these were 'documents that would not pass the British postal authorities'.[8] She also returned to Dublin a few times in late 1916, but eventually decided to go to America, both to visit her brother, Thomas, and to join Nora Connolly and the other revolutionary women who were there on a propaganda tour.

On 1 December 1916 Skinnider began her journey to New York. The previous autumn she had hosted the bereaved Irish woman Hanna Sheehy Skeffington and her son, Owen, in her home in Glasgow. Sheehy Skeffington was a well-known militant suffragette and nationalist. Her husband, Francis, had been shot without trial in Portobello Barracks during the Rising. After the

Rising, Mrs Sheehy Skeffington had insisted on an official inquiry into the circumstances of her husband's death, and while she succeeded in getting this, the full report was not published. Her dissatisfaction at the behaviour of the British authorities, and a desire for justice for her husband and for Ireland, drove her to seek satisfaction in America. Legally she was not allowed to travel without a government permit, but thanks to friends in Scotland, including Skinnider, she managed to get a permit in the identity of a Mrs Gribben, a Scotswoman, and with that she travelled to America just before Christmas 1916.[9] Several other women who had fought in 1916 also travelled to America. These journeys were part of the propaganda roles undertaken by advanced nationalist women in the post-1916 period. In months after the Rising, with much of the male leadership of the Irish Volunteers dead or in jail, it was up to the women to re-organise as 'only the women remained free to consolidate the new mood and generate a new movement; it all depended on their energy and their commitment'.[10] The immediate need was to fundraise money to support those who had been directly affected by the Rising; widows and their families whose husbands were killed or executed, and the families of those men held in prison camps who were now bereft, emotionally and financially. Cumann na mBan women, such as the newly widowed Kathleen Clarke, whose husband, Tom, had been executed, threw themselves into fundraising for the newly formed organisations, the Irish Volunteers' Dependants' Fund (IVDF) and the Irish National Aid Association (INAA).[11]

As important as fundraising was, propaganda was also very important. Initial public reactions to Easter Week were not favourable, either locally or internationally, and in the months following the Rising the women of Cumann na mBan organised effective republican propaganda campaigns. Skinnider mentioned one source of effective propaganda in her memoir. These were the 'wives, mothers and daughters of the men executed or sentenced for life'.[12] Cumann na mBan recognised the power of the images of these men and women. They were soon producing and disseminating Easter Week memorabilia, postcards, and posters which commemorated the executed and imprisoned men of 1916. They submitted articles to newspapers describing the heroics and sacrifice of the patriot dead. The widows and mothers of 1916, especially the widows of the executed signatories, were also very effective symbols of the sacrifices of the men. A gendered concept of sacrifice was used in these propaganda campaigns, and it fell on fertile ground. In a culture already attuned to the concept of the heroic male fighting and dying for 'Mother Ireland', images of the dead, male, patriots of 1916 re-enforced the relationship between patriotism, militancy and masculinity. Republican womanhood, on the other hand, was portrayed in this propaganda as passive. A potent example of these passive images of patriotic women were those produced in the *Catholic Bulletin* in December 1916.[13] Áine Ceannt, Muriel McDonagh, Lillie Connolly, Agnes Mallin and Kathleen Clarke were photographed in their widows' weeds, surrounded by their orphaned children. Hanna Sheehy Skeffington, widow of the murdered Francis, was photographed with her son, Owen, while Nannie O'Rahilly was photographed with her four sons, one of whom, Rory, had been born in July 1916, three months after the death of his father, Irish Volunteer leader, Michael O'Rahilly, known as 'The' O'Rahilly. Mrs Pearse, mother of the executed Patrick and William, was also included.[14] In particular, the poignant image of Grace Gifford and 1916 leader, Joseph Plunkett, resonated; the story of how the young couple married in Kilmainham Gaol two hours before he was executed was widely publicised and articles about their marriage appeared in Irish, English, and American newspapers.

The Bulletin was very important in moulding the growing post-Rising support of the ideologies of the rebels.[15] It was, as Sinn Féin historian P. S. O'Hegarty later admitted, one of the papers which helped 'make the Rising acceptable to a majority in Ireland'.[16] However, it was not the only type of propaganda that the women were able to undertake. While these pamphlets, articles and photographs of the patriot men and the mourning women were very effective in Ireland, it was also important to counteract British propaganda internationally, especially among the large Irish-American population in the United States. Soon after the Rising, republican women began to leave for America with the intention of spreading the truth of what happened in Ireland during Easter Week. Eye-witness testimonies and accounts were important and designed to raise much needed funds, highlight the suffering of men and women of 1916 and their families, and 'inspire emotional sympathy for the rebels' cause'.[17] Bringing these stories and reports to America was the work, initially, of the women. Among those who travelled were Min Ryan, Nellie Gifford, Hanna Sheehy Skeffington, Margaret Skinnider and Nora Connolly. Connolly went in August 1916 and Skinnider travelled to New York in December. She arrived a week before Hanna Sheehy Skeffington and, with Connolly, met her off the boat, when she and her son Owen, arrived in New York. Sheehy Skeffington would, in her 18-month stay in America, speak at more than 250 functions.[18] It is unknown how many meetings Skinnider and Connolly addressed, but both addressed dozens of meetings and did 'propaganda work' and fundraising on behalf of the INAAVDF.[19]

Skinnider and Connolly shared a home in New York and, although they travelled widely in America, their home base was in Brooklyn. Skinnider's brother Thomas was already living there and they were in frequent contact with him. It is obvious from references to him in the memoirs of ICA man, Frank Robbins, that Thomas was as involved in republican activities as his sister. On his arrival in New York Robbins sought out Thomas, who then introduced him to several of the revolutionary Irish and Irish-American activists in the city. Among them was Robert Monteith, who, along with Roger Casement, had been part of the attempt to smuggle arms into Kerry before the Rising. Unlike Casement, he had evaded arrest and escaped to America. More importantly, Thomas introduced Robbins to the old Fenian John Devoy, who was the head of Clan na Gael in New York.[20] This meant when Margaret Skinnider arrived in New York in December 1916 she already had close connections among the revolutionary Irish emigrants, as well as among the politically engaged Irish-American population. Along with her brother and Robbins, Nora Connolly was there, as was Connolly's most senior revolutionary contact, Liam Mellows. Mellows was a republican and a socialist well known to both James and Nora Connolly. He was a member of the IRB and the Irish Volunteers. Prior to the Rising, he was working at re-organising the Volunteers in Galway. Because of this work he was arrested under the Defence of the Realm Act (DORA) and deported to Leek in Staffordshire. When plans for the Rising were being finalised it was important to get Mellows back to Ireland, and this job fell to Nora Connolly. Connolly used her contacts in Scotland, particularly in Glasgow, to secrete Mellows, disguised as a priest, back to Ireland. Mellows then led the Rising in Galway, but unlike so many of his comrades, he managed to evade arrest and took a boat to New York. There he contacted Devoy and Clan na Gael and was, by 1917, working for Devoy's paper, *The Gaelic American*, writing articles on the Fianna and the Easter Rising, through Nora Connolly, Skinnider, Mellows and Robbins met and worked together in New York.

Nora Connolly later said of her time in America that as soon as she arrived, she was 'whirled off as a propagandist'.[21] When Skinnider joined her in December 1916, the whirlwind tours continued. They did not have to get jobs immediately, as the

INAAVDF supported them by paying their living and travel expenses so they could concentrate on their talks and on their writing, as both were producing eye-witness accounts of their experiences in the Rising. Although Connolly felt she was never cut out to be a public speaker, she found that Irish Americans 'hung on every syllable', as they wanted to hear the story [of 1916] told in 'my own words'.[22] The women spoke to sell-out crowds of thousands in New York, Boston, Philadelphia, Chicago, and many other cities. Connolly recalled seeing John Butler Yeats (father of W. B. Yeats) in New York after a talk she gave. He said to her, she recalled, 'I bow to the maiden who has obtained millions of pounds for the Irish cause, without extending anything but her voice'.[23] However, Connolly was suddenly stricken with appendicitis, and retired from public speaking to do a university course in Boston in the winter and spring of 1917.[24] She started up again in the summer of 1917 and travelled, like Skinnider, all over the country.

In January 1918, both Connolly and Skinnider visited Washington where they managed to meet Jeannette Rankin of Montana, the first woman to be elected to the House of Congress. To the militant suffragette Skinnider, meeting a woman who had been elected to national political office would have been inspiring. Rankin was also very supportive of the Irish cause, stating 'a common bond of sympathy makes the Suffragists and the Irish the best fighters for Democracy today'.[25] That January Hanna Sheehy Skeffington managed to get into the White House to see President Woodrow Wilson where she presented him with a petition:

> signed by Constance Markievicz in her capacity as President of Cumann na mBan, by Margaret, mother of Patrick and William Pearse, by Jennie Wyse Power and many other Irish women, putting forward the claim of Ireland for self-determination and appealing to President Wilson to include Ireland among the small nations for whose freedom America was fighting.[26]

Back in New York both Skinnider and Connolly were involved in activities with Clan na Gael and, particularly, with Liam Mellows and Frank Robbins. Mellows had come up with a plan to re-arm the Volunteers by buying arms from Germany and smuggling them to Ireland. Robbins was also involved in this plan, which was ultimately unsuccessful. However, as he was under surveillance, Mellows was arrested on charges of conspiring to impersonate an American seaman and imprisoned in New York's infamous Tombs Prison (this was the colloquial name for the Manhattan Detention Complex). While there, he was visited by Skinnider and Connolly, who, in order to circumvent the listening guards, spoke to him in Irish and 'discovered he had hidden [papers] behind a picture in the dining room' of the house he was lodging in.[27] With this information the women went to the house and managed to retrieve the incriminating papers.

The Irish republican women were very effective on their speaking tours, so much so that they came to the attention of the authorities and were often under surveillance. While the Irish American crowds were huge and receptive, there was also a lot of pro-war politicising as well as pro-war propaganda in the media as the British Government was intensifying its campaign to have America join the war. So threatening were the public lectures given by the Irish republican women that the British Ambassador requested that Sheehy Skeffington be sent home as a 'dangerous agitator'.[28] An American official, the Postmaster General, A.G. Burleson, called her 'the worst of Irish agitators now here', and noted that her speeches were of a 'most violent and incendiary character'.[29] Another of the women on the tour, Min Ryan, was arrested for selling Irish Republican flags; she was released on a suspended sentence.[30] But Irish-American nationalism was stirring and anxious to hear more of the Rising and the truth about the conditions in Ireland. Skinnider, Connolly, Sheehy Skeffington, and the others provided this and, according to Father Peter Yorke, a member of Friends of Irish Freedom (FOIF), Sheehy Skeffington [and the others] were 'finally successful in convincing many millions of American people that Ireland is entitled to her independence'.[31]

In her 'Account of Eighteen Months Irish Propaganda in the United States', Hanna Sheehy Skeffington paid due regard to the talks which the 'Irish refugees' of Easter Week gave, and to the books they produced. Among them she listed '*Ireland's Tragic Easter*, edited by Mr. Padraic Colum; *The Sinn Féin Movement*, by Mr Frank Jones; … Later, Miss Margaret Skinnider's book entitled *Doing My Bit for Ireland*, and Miss Nora Connolly's *The Unbroken Tradition*'.[32] Skinnider's *Doing My Bit for Ireland* was published in New York in June 1917 by the Century Company. The book was a chronicle of her life leading up to and during the Rising of 1916. Eye-witness accounts of the Rising were in demand with Irish-American audiences and *Doing My Bit for Ireland* was well received, despite what some considered its rather brusque writing style.[33] Blending the personal and the political, Skinnider concentrated on her activities with Na Fianna and the Irish Volunteers in Scotland, and her encounters with Markievicz and Connolly in Dublin, before providing a day-by-day account of the Rising from the perspective of the garrison in the Royal College of Surgeons (RCSI). She also outlined the reasons, as she understood them, why the Irish rose in rebellion including the oppression experienced by people, like her forebears in Monaghan, under British rule, and the extreme poverty experienced by the working class in Dublin.

Gender is central, and complex, in *Doing My Bit for Ireland*. Skinnider writes little of Cumann na mBan, the organisation of which she was an official member. Indeed, Cumann na mBan is the organisation she was to be very involved with through the War of Independence and Civil War. However, in *Doing My Bit for Ireland*, she barely mentions Cumann na mBan, other than she joined the Anne Devlin Branch in Glasgow in 1915. Her work with Na Fianna, training the boys and passing as one of them in Dublin, was more important at this stage of her life as a militant, so much so that she included a photograph of herself in a Fianna uniform. In a 1917 letter to John O'Donnell, she proudly boasts of 'her boys' in Glasgow who did their bit and promised to show him a photograph of them.[34] She spends time describing her abilities to pass in many roles, as a Fianna boy, as a girl messenger, and as a uniformed sniper. She consciously inhabited these different roles in a gendered fashion. This 'gender mimicry' does suggest that, for some activist women, part of the attraction of revolutionary activism was 'because it permitted unorthodox modes of behaviour'.[35] Like her mentor, Markievicz, Skinnider was aware of the how dress altered what roles she could play. She described Markievicz as she saw her on the Green, at the start of the Rising: 'The Countess stood motionless ... She was a lieutenant in the Irish Volunteers and, in her officer's uniform and black hat with great plumes, looked most impressive.'[36] Both Skinnider and Markievicz disrupted, in many ways, the traditional gender order with their dress and actions during the Easter Rising. However, they also both showed an understanding of masculinity and militarism, as it was only in male dress that they, as women, could really be soldiers. When Skinnider took up her gun or led a military action, she was in her moleskin uniform; when she was on her bicycle delivering dispatches, she was in her grey dress. The book also 'provides one of the most vivid, and poetic, descriptions of what kind of courage was necessary to be an activist woman during Easter Week'.[37] The bravery shown by Skinnider and Markievicz is front and centre, but so too is the bravery of the Red Cross 'girls', the women she admired, Kathleen Lynn and Helena Molony, and the other dispatch carriers, such as Irish Citizen Army woman and

RCSI garrison member, Chris Caffrey, who was stopped and strip-searched by the British.[38]

Even with its unorthodox approach to gender *Doing My Bit for Ireland* received popular and critical attention. In fact, the photograph of Skinnider in male dress was used to promote the book. Irish-American audiences enjoyed the tales of bravery and tragedy, particularly from a participant who had suffered her own wounds. The book was published in an attractive style, 'bound in green with an embossed Celtic Cross in gold on the front cover ... and ... included photographs of Constance Markievicz, James Connolly, and Margaret Skinnider, as well as Pearse's Proclamation of the Irish Republic'. It was priced at one dollar, making it accessible to a wide readership.[39] It was reviewed, mostly favourably, in respected publications such as *The Dial*, *The Nation* and *The New York Times Book Review*.[40] Comparing the Rising to the World War (still ongoing, and which America was about to join), the reviewer in *The Dial* felt that the book had all the 'qualities of drama – excitement, irony, beauty which the world war seems to lack'.[41] While one reviewer called the book 'naïve', most were laudatory, and, as *The Dial* reviewer wrote:

> Miss Skinnider's simple recital is that it makes the Irish revolutionaries live for us, especially their executed leaders, so that the Irish question presents itself as an essentially human problem and the rights of small nations changes for a battle cry to a demand for constructive thought.[42]

The Detroit Times, in its review, felt that much of the story of the revolution had not been told in the Press in America and 'had Miss Skinnider not done what she did, it is not too much to say that America would never have understood the indomitable spirit which animated these Irish patriots'.[43] Dorothy Day, journalist, social activist and co-founder of *The Catholic Worker*, also reviewed the book, noting that the book's attractiveness was that it made the Rising seem 'so homelike', and that 'we now have the true facts of the unfortunately unsuccessful rising'.[44]

After the publication of *Doing My Bit for Ireland*, Skinnider and Connolly continued their propaganda work. Connolly's account of the Rising, *The Unbroken Tradition*, was published in 1918, but banned in America as prejudicial to the wartime alliance with Britain. By late 1917, neither Skinnider nor Connolly were happy to remain much longer in America. Skinnider was worried about her father, as he was ill, and she fretted about not being able to help her mother care for him. He died in October of that year and she was unable to be at his funeral. Also, as she said in a letter to her friend, Julia Fraher Rohan, 'I don't like N. Y. at all'.[45] In another letter to Fraher Rohan Nora Connolly complained that she was 'dying with the heat'.[46] Skinnider had earlier been, according to a report in *The Gaelic American*, employed in Washington 'on special work on which she was an expert', but that had come to an end and she was back in New York.[47] They were, at all times, aware of what was happening in Ireland and were delighted, as Connolly wrote to Fraher Rohan in 1917, that 'de Valera had won the elections 3 to 1'.[48] They missed the joyous occasions when the Irish prisoners were finally released from prison camps in 1917, including Skinnider's mentor and comrade, Countess Markievicz. Skinnider would also have been aware that the Representation of People Act had passed. This allowed women, albeit only those over the age of 30 with certain property qualification, the right to vote. They would have also heard from letters and visitors from Ireland of the country-wide anti-conscription campaigns, which began in April 1918, in which the women of the IWWU, the ICA and Cumann na mBan played very important roles.

They were getting very anxious to return home, as was Hanna Sheehy Skeffington. All three, Skinnider, Connolly and Sheehy

Skeffington, had difficulty getting passports to travel, but they eventually secured them, although they were only allowed to travel as far as Liverpool in England. In June 1918, the women prepared to depart New York. Hanna Sheehy Skeffington described their leave taking:

> Our boat left New York on June 27, 1918. We were seen off by Liam Mellows & others very carefully searched, had to strip to our skin & take down my hair; female searchers of a very hard type … I was bringing money for the organisation home – later I handed it to Collins whom I met for the first time in Dublin in August. … We were four (Nora [Connolly], Margaret [Skinnider], Owen and self & had a four-berth cabin. …When we docked in Liverpool the fun began for us four. We were kept apart from the rest & searched separately & our luggage 'combed'.[49]

After arriving in Liverpool, they were held and questioned. Sheehy Skeffington was not allowed travel on to Ireland; Skinnider and Connolly, because of their Scottish birth, were allowed continue to Glasgow. Skinnider and the other republican women had worked hard and successfully as propagandists in America. *The Gaelic American* wrote of Hanna Sheehy Skeffington, 'Mrs. Skeffington has done more real good to the cause of Ireland during her short stay in America that all the Irish orators and writers who have undertaken to enlighten the American people for the past twenty-five years.'[50]

As Sheehy Skeffington noted in an unpublished memoir, when the women docked in Liverpool, 'the fun began'.[51] All three were taken separately and questioned while their baggage was searched; even young Owen was questioned. While Sheehy Skeffington was again expressly forbidden to return to Ireland for 'the duration of the war', Connolly and Skinnider were 'going to Glasgow and passed on'.[52] All three were regarded as dangerous. The Commander-in-Chief of the British Forces in Ireland had already stated that if 'these three ladies … enter Ireland they will undoubtedly at once become, if not active agitators, figureheads for the encouragement of disloyal propaganda'.[53] Obviously news of their successful propaganda tours had reached Dublin. Sheehy Skeffington was to spend some time in Liverpool until, in August, she secretly took a boat back to Dublin. In Glasgow, Connolly discovered that the Dublin Castle authorities had decided that it was 'inimical to the peace of this Realm to allow Nora Connolly reside in Ireland'.[54] Frustrated with this, she made up her mind to get back to Dublin using subterfuge. Connolly had also used male attire to go about her business before the Rising, and she used it again to leave England. She decided to stowaway on a boat sailing for Dublin from Birkenhead, where her contacts told her to 'dress up as a boy and we will take you'.[55] A 'good suit' of a boy named Hicks from Waterford was found, which fitted except for the trousers, an issue she solved by 'taking my scarf, I wound it round like a *crois*, and with that I held [it] up'. Dressed in her male attire, the men smiled and noted that 'it is a cocky young fellow we have with us'.[56] Although she had some nerve-wracking encounters with policemen and sailors on her way to the boat, Connolly successfully arrived back in Ireland.

Meanwhile, back in Glasgow, Skinnider lived with her widowed mother and reconnected with her sisters Mary and Isabelle, who were schoolteachers in Glasgow and her brother Joseph, who was a merchant seaman.[57] She also got some teaching work in August, in St John's Public School, Glasgow.[58] Like many of her revolutionary comrades, however, she soon threw herself back into militant activism. She re-joined the local Anne Devlin Branch of Cumann na mBan and became their captain. Like many branches of Cumann na mBan, it had fallen into disarray after the Rising,

but had been re-organised in 1917, while the membership continued
to be 'overwhelmingly young and unmarried and a large number
of them were schoolteachers'.[59] The branch had recommenced
training, and Skinnider taught them First Aid and drill. She also
helped organise other branches of Cumann na mBan in the city,
and gave them training in 'the use of small arms'.[60] She and
Cumann na mBan worked closely with the Irish Republican Army
(IRA, the name the Irish Volunteers were now using), which had
also been reorganised in Glasgow: 'being a smaller group we
[Glasgow Cumann na mBan] worked more closely in conjunction
with the IRA than here [Ireland]'.[61] Much of that work she under-
took was similar to her pre-1916 activities. She participated in
raids for small arms, in raids on collieries seeking explosives, as
well as transporting and storing the stolen material.[62] By 1919 the
Skinnider family were living at 14 Kersland Street, in Glasgow, a
wealthy part of the city 'not under suspicion – there were not many
Irish people living in the place', so she was safely able to store and
transport arms.[63] Interestingly, Kersland Street was not far from
the Botanic Gardens where Skinnider's suffragette comrades had
bombed the glasshouse in 1914 as part of their militant suffrage
campaign. However, she wanted, like Connolly and Sheehy
Skeffington, to return to Dublin. Skinnider arrived back in March
1919 and contacted her Cumann na mBan comrades almost
immediately.

CHAPTER FOUR

Margaret and Nóra
At Home and at War

While they were in America, both Margaret Skinnider and Nora Connolly met two people who were to be very important in their lives. Connolly met Seamus O'Brien, a commercial traveller, who was active in the War of Independence as a courier for Michael Collins. She married O'Brien in 1922, adopting the surname Connolly O'Brien, which she went by for the rest of her life. Skinnider met Nóra O'Keeffe, with whom she would live, in Dublin, from 1919 until O'Keeffe died in 1961. The O'Keeffe's were from Glenough Lower, Clonoulty in County Tipperary, where she was born in 1885, the sixth of twelve children born to Daniel and Ellen (née Ryan) O'Keeffe. The family were well-to-do farmers and educated their children in the local school. They were also involved in the Gaelic League and immersed in cultural nationalism. O'Keeffe signed herself Nóra Ní Chaoimh (the Irish version of her name) in most of her correspondence throughout her life. Aged 24, Nóra travelled to New York in 1909, with her older brother Patrick, and remained there for the next 10 years. As her family were very sympathetic to the cause of Irish freedom, it is likely she had dealings with the politicised Irish emigrants and Irish Americans in Clan na Gael in New York. It is unknown how and when she and Skinnider met, but by 1919 they were both back in Dublin, living together, at first in Fairview and later in Clontarf.

Their first home was in Waverley Avenue, in Fairview, and both soon joined the Fairview Branch of Cumann na mBan.[1] Skinnider already knew some of the members of the Fairview branch as they had been with her in the RCSI during the Rising. By the time Skinnider and O'Keeffe were working with the Fairview branch, a lot had changed, politically, in Ireland. The World War was over, and a General Election had been held in December 1918. In this election, Sinn Féin the political wing of the IRA, had won an overwhelming majority, and Skinnider's old friend, Countess Markievicz, had become the first woman elected to the House of Commons. As a member of Sinn Féin, Markievicz had not taken her Commons seat. In January 1919, although still in Holloway Jail, she had become the first woman TD in the First Dáil, which met on 21 January, in the Mansion House in Dublin. By April 1919, she was Minister for Labour, again a first for a woman in Ireland. Irish nationalist politics had transformed since 1916. The Redmonite Home Rule Party and its constitutional nationalist ideology was losing support, as most of the population had swung behind Sinn Féin and their desire for an independent Ireland. Part of the reason for the 'greening of Irish politics' post-1916 was due to the successful propaganda and anti-conscription campaigns undertaken by the women of Cumann na mBan, the IWWU, and the ICA in 1917 and 1918.

Sinn Féin had fought the election of 1918 on an abstentionist policy, a promise to convene an Irish parliament in Dublin, and to go to the peace talks in Versailles to persuade negotiators there that Ireland was one of the 'small nations' which deserved its independence. At the same time fundraising to reorganise and re-arm militant groups such as Cumann an mBan and the IRA continued. And those arms were soon needed. On 21 January, 1919 as the First Dáil met in the Mansion House in Dublin, one of the first engagements of the War of Independence occurred at Soloheadbeg in

County Tipperary. Here, IRA men led by Séumas Robinson (a comrade of Skinnider's from Glasgow), Seán Treacy (a cousin of Nóra O'Keeffe), Dan Breen, commandant of the Third Tipperary Brigade, and others from the Third Tipperary Brigade of the IRA, aided by the women of Cumann na mBan, attacked a wagon coming from the local quarry. The wagon was loaded with gelignite which the IRA men wanted to steal and was guarded by two RIC constables. In the ambush the two RIC men were killed and war in Ireland was now a reality. Skinnider and republican men and women in Scotland had already responded to the outbreak of hostilities in January 1919 with further raids for arms and explosives in Glasgow; transporting, when they could, this material to the IRA in Ireland. When Skinnider arrived in Dublin in March she wanted to continue her work with the IRA and with Cumann na mBan.

Skinnider and O'Keeffe would play integral roles in the War of Independence over the coming years, as members of Cumann na mBan. O'Keeffe's republican family was also very involved. Two of her brothers, Dan and Con, were in the IRA and her sisters 'gave of their best', particularly her younger sister Brigid, who was Captain of the local Clonulty branch of Cumann na mBan.[2] Séan Hogan, one of the IRA men involved in Soloheadbeg, had spent time in the O'Keeffe safe house and was, reputedly, 'in love with Bridie O'Keeffe of Glenough'.[3] In May 1919 Hogan was captured by the British and imprisoned in Thurles, County Tipperary. The local IRA got news that Hogan was about to be moved by the British forces, from Thurles to Cork. The leaders of the Third Tipperary Brigade, including Breen, Robinson, Treacy and Padraig Kinane, held a 'council of war at the O'Keeffe home, where all the plans to get Seán [Hogan] out of the hands of his foes' were made.[4] They decided, in cooperation with the East Limerick Brigade of the IRA and aided by local Cumann na mBan women, to hold up

the train and rescue Hogan at Knocklong, County Limerick. On
13 May, the train was hijacked at Knocklong. The action succeeded, Hogan was rescued, although not without the deaths of
two of the RIC officers guarding Hogan, while several IRA men
were wounded including Treacy and Breen.

After Knocklong the men of the Third Tipperary Brigade were
constantly on the run, often taking shelter at the O'Keeffe safe
house in Glenough. Breen and Treacy had to leave Tipperary
periodically, and both made their way to Dublin. In Dublin, Treacy
became involved in the unsuccessful attempts to assassinate the
Irish Viceroy, Lord French, and the then Chief Secretary, Sir Ian
Macpherson. Moving between Dublin and Tipperary, he proved a
thorn in the side of the authorities. When in Dublin he sometimes
visited his 'friend Nora O'Keeffe', proving that she was implicitly
trusted by the IRA.[5] In October 1920 he called in to see her at
Liberty Hall, where she was working as a secretary to Thomas
Johnson, Leader of the Labour Party. But the British authorities,
working with spies, informers and the local secret service agents,
were at this point closing in on Treacy. A few days after his visit
with O'Keeffe, while he was hiding at a safe house, Fernside, in
Drumcondra, with Dan Breen, the attack came. The house was
surrounded and Breen and Treacy had to shoot their way out.
During the firefight two of the British intelligence officers were
killed. Breen and Treacy escaped but were hunted men. As 'Miss
O'Keeffe knew, [and] all of Treacy's friends knew, … he was determined never to be taken alive'.[6] There was a plan formulated
to attack senior British military personnel at the funeral, on 14
October, of the intelligence officers killed at Fernside, but when
these senior military personnel did not appear, the plan was
aborted. Treacy, however, had been spotted standing in a doorway
on Talbot Street, and in an exchange of fire, he and a British
intelligence officer were killed.

This was a major propaganda coup for the British authorities, they had managed to track down and kill one of the notorious 'Big Four' IRA men: Breen, Hogan, Treacy and Robinson. The police removed the body to the King George V Hospital where Nóra O'Keeffe volunteered to go and 'place the matter beyond any doubt that it was indeed Seán Treacy'.[7] Like so many Cumann na mBan women were to do during the War of Independence, O'Keeffe now had to perform the difficult task of identifying the bloodied body of a young man whom she knew well, with whom she was good friends, a man who was her cousin and her revolutionary comrade. 'She wept' as she identified the 'fine looking man', overcome by 'all the memories of [Treacy] alive in the O'Keeffe home in Glenough'.[8] She borrowed a scissors from the hovering soldier and cut off a lock of his hair, and also took his ring for safe keeping. On 16 October Treacy's remains were then removed to the Pro-Cathedral in Dublin, where they lay overnight. They were then taken by train from Kingsbridge Station in Dublin to Limerick Junction and escorted from there, by a huge crowd, to Solohead Church where the funeral mass took place. Treacy was buried in Kilfeakle Graveyard, where, despite a large British presence, a volley of shots was fired over his grave.

As the revolutionary war intensified in later 1920 and into 1921 Skinnider and O'Keeffe continued their activities in Cumann na mBan. In their home in Fairview they 'kept people on the run' and stored arms, indeed Skinnider later recalled that she could not 'remember a time when [she] was not storing arms'.[9] O'Keeffe was a trained typist and stenographer, and these skills were of use in her work as a dispatch carrier. She was well connected with Tipperary Cumann na mBan and IRA and spent time in both Dublin, Tipperary and other areas of Munster on Cumann na mBan work. Skinnider mostly worked in Dublin, taking guns to ambushes, delivering dispatches and working on fundraising, as she had in America. She collected and distributed money 'practically every evening' for the Dependants' Fund, as well as conducting drilling, training and giving lectures on First Aid to the Fairview and other Cumann na mBan branches.[10] 1921 was not an easy time for either woman. As well as the danger of their work as part of Cumann na mBan, both experienced personal tragedies. In May 1921 the O'Keeffe home in Glenough was blown up by the Black and Tans. Denis O'Keeffe (Fr Benedict), one of Nóra's uncles, wrote to his brother Michael in Australia, with details of what happened:

> there was no one in the house when the Military Lorries arrived but the youngest girl and her mother … They [the women] were allowed to remove to a safe place, clothes and foodstuffs, but no furniture was allowed to be removed, all was destroyed … The parlour with all in it was totally destroyed. It seems Dan and Mrs Dan kept up their courage. They are hoping for better times. Patriotism was the only charge against them.[11]

When the Black and Tans arrived to blow the house up, their brother Con was there, but his sister, Clonulty Cumann na mBan Captain, Brigid, acting as a scout, gave a warning and he escaped out the back. As the military truck arrived, the girls (Nóra's younger sisters) 'ran away for fear of the brutal soldiery', while their mother, although ill in bed, was given an hour to pack what she could and get out.[12] In spite of this trauma, the resilience of the family was noted by IRA man, Michael Davern, who visited the house soon after the attack:

> when we called at O'Keeffe's at Glenough, we found Mrs and Mr O'Keeffe, who were then very old people, sitting in an old barn which had not been blown up. They said: 'So long as a hair of your head is not touched, we don't mind. Let the old house go to blazes!'[13]

Despite this, both O'Keeffe and Skinnider continued their work in Cumann na mBan until the Truce was called in July 1921. Like many other members of the organisation, they were waiting on the outcome of negotiations and continued to drill and train with their branch in Fairview. In October 1921 Skinnider was co-opted on to the Executive of Cumann na mBan and appointed Director of Training for the whole organisation. She was, as Kathleen Clarke, noted, 'one of the most efficient members and an untiring worker, and held in the highest esteem by the Executive and the branches in which she was a member'.[14]

However, tragedy was to strike the Skinnider/O'Keeffe household again. Skinnider's mother, Jane, widowed since 1918, often visited and stayed with her daughter at Waverley Avenue in Fairview. On Saturday night, 8 October 1921, Mrs Skinnider, again coming to visit Dublin, boarded the SS *Rowan* in Glasgow. Shortly after midnight, sailing in dense fog, the *Rowan* was involved in a double collision. Over a ten-minute period, in very poor visibility, she was struck by two vessels, the American steamer *West Camak*, which hit her astern, and then the British steamer *Clan Malcolm*, which rammed her from starboard and cut her in two. She sunk very quickly after the second collision, off Corsewall Point near Stranraer. Although there was no passenger list kept, it is believed that there were about 90 people on board that night, of whom, 25 passengers and eleven crew members were drowned. Among those missing and presumed drowned was Mrs Jane Skinnider. On 12 October, *The Freemans Journal* reported that a telegram received in Dublin stated that 'Mrs Skinnider, 31 Waverely Avenue, Fairview, was with Mrs Rennichan and the latter's daughter up to the second collision'.[15] Mrs Rennichan was thrown clear during that collision and saved, but her daughter and Mrs Skinnider were not seen since. The same day *The Scotsman* reported that a Mrs Skinnider, 14 Kersland Street, Glasgow, was among the missing.[16] Five days later, on Monday, 17 October, her body washed ashore at Machrihanish, Argyllshire, and 'her son and two daughters left Dublin for Glasgow where internment was to take place'.[17] In the space of three years, Margaret Skinnider had lost both her parents, but at least, this time, she could attend the funeral of her mother. The requiem mass was held in St Joseph's Church in Glasgow where the celebrant spoke of Mrs Skinnider as a 'person full of kindness and sympathy for others' and of her 'great self-sacrifice and kindness to those in trouble or distress'. On the deck of the *Rowan* she was said to have spent her last minutes comforting those in danger with no thought 'for her own danger'.[18]

There were several interesting aspects to the sinking of the *SS Rowan*. A report on the sinking, sent to the British authorities in Ireland, noted that it was suspected that 'a certain amount of arms, etc for the IRA are said to have gone down on the *SS Rowan*'.[19] Even though the Truce was holding the IRA was rearming, and republicans in Scotland were, as they had been since before 1916, involved in this. This would not have been unusual or unexpected. The smuggling of arms and munitions from Scotland had begun well before 1916 and would continue through the War of Independence and into the Civil War. Another interesting aspect of the War Office report is more unexpected. In the same report it was stated that:

a Mrs Skinnider was one of the passengers downed on the S. S. Rowan, she was accompanied by a Miss Keeffe (or O'Keeffe), who is said to be one of the most notorious despatch [*sic*] riders, IRA in Ireland. This girl is said to carry despatches [*sic*] between Dublin, Cork, Kerry, Tipperary and Waterford.[20]

While Nóra O'Keeffe's name does not appear in any newspaper report as a survivor of the sinking, and there was no extant passenger list, there is no reason to believe that she was not on the *Rowan* with Mrs Skinnider. The depiction of her as one of the 'most notorious despatch [*sic*] riders', indicates that her work had brought her to the attention of the authorities. While earlier in the war Dublin Castle and the intelligence authorities might not have recognised the importance of Cumann na mBan to the activities of the IRA in fighting what was a guerrilla war, by 1921 they had become more aware of the importance of the women. As Lil Conlin, a member of Cork Cumann na mBan, later wrote, by late 1920:

> attention was focussed on the Women very much at this time by the Authorities, they were in receipt of information from their Intelligence Division, owing to raids and capture of documents, and they realised fully that Women were playing a major part in the Campaign.[21]

Resulting from their work, many of the women of Cumann na mBan experienced the worst of the raids and reprisals on their homes from mid-1920 until the truce was called in July 1921, when 'masked raiders could come to threaten, bully and burn out their homes'.[22] The experience of the O'Keeffe family of having their home burned to the ground was replicated throughout the country. Active Cumann na mBan women were also targeted; they could not usually go on the run as their male comrades did, and reprisals were often directed at them. They were subjected to violent midnight raids, where they were dragged out of their beds, beaten up, manhandled or worse. This include both physical and sexual assault, many had their hair roughly sheared, others reported assaults committed against their person. While the word rape was rarely used, words such as indignity, assault or outrage committed against them indicate the brutal experiences of many women. However, like Skinnider and O'Keeffe, neither trauma nor tragedy stopped most of the women from continuing their work for Ireland.

A truce between the armed forces in Ireland had come into effect on 11 July 1921, with the IRA and Cumann na mBan on ceasefire for the rest of 1921. Negotiations between the President of the Irish Executive, Éamon de Valera, and British Prime Minister, David Lloyd George, began, and continued via letters and meetings until October when Michael Collins led the Irish plenipotentiaries to London to negotiate and sign a treaty. Interestingly, despite its contribution to the war, Cumann na mBan had no representative among the delegation to London. Early on 6 December 1921, the Irish plenipotentiaries signed the 'Articles of Agreement for a Treaty between Great Britain and Ireland'. The Treaty offered less than the Republic that the women of Cumann na mBan had been fighting for. The island was to remain partitioned with the six counties of Northern Ireland remaining within the United Kingdom. An Irish Free State with a parliament in Dublin, albeit with dominion status within the United Kingdom, was to be formed in the other 26 counties. All members of future Irish parliaments in Dublin would be required to take an Oath of Allegiance to the British monarch, who would still be represented in the Free State by a Governor General. When news of the contents of the Anglo-Irish Treaty reached Dublin consternation and division among republican organisations, male and female, ensued.

Cumann na mBan were the first to call a meeting of their executive and a convention of their membership to discuss the Treaty. All six women TDs had, during the Dáil debates, already rejected the Treaty. By mid-January 1922, the Executive of Cumann na mBan (which included Skinnider) had affirmed its anti-Treaty stance, stating that 'the executive of Cumann na mBan reaffirms their allegiance to the Irish Republic and therefore cannot support the Articles of Treaty signed in London'.[23] A convention of the Cumann na mBan membership was called for 5 February 1922 to debate a resolution put forward by Mary MacSwiney, 'reaffirming allegiance to the Republic and calling upon the Women of Ireland to support in forthcoming elections only those candidates who stood true to the existing Republic proclaimed Easter Week, 1916'.[24] Several of Skinnider's old colleagues were pro-Treaty, including Jennie Wyse Power and Min Mulcahy (née Ryan). While Mulcahy and Wyse Power defended the Treaty as a stepping stone to full independence, most attendees at the convention remained resolutely anti-Treaty. Skinnider, in her contribution to the debate, said it was

> not a question between the Republic and the Free State. It [was] a question between the Republic and the British Empire ... Mrs Wyse Power asks are we going to oppose an Irish Government? Once a man takes an Oath of Allegiance to England, he is no longer an Irishman in my opinion.[25]

The anti-Treaty women carried the convention convincingly, and Cumann na mBan, as an organisation, was now in opposition to the Irish Government in Dublin.

Interestingly, suffrage issues resurfaced at this time. The upcoming election, called for June 1922, would secure (or not) the Treaty position. In that election, under existing laws, all men over the age of 21 but only women over the age of 30 could vote. During the Dáil debates the anti-Treaty women TDs argued that all women over the age of 21 should be given the vote, on a par with men, as promised by the Proclamation. Despite the assurance that equal suffrage for men and women would be in the new Free State constitution, it was argued that the new electoral register would not be ready in time for the upcoming June election.[26] Many political women felt this was simply an excuse to not have women under 30 vote, as it was presumed that many younger women would be anti-Treaty. This meant that, as in 1918, and 1921, only women over the age of 30, with certain property qualifications, could vote. Margaret Skinnider was 30 in 1922 and Nóra O'Keeffe was 37, although it is not known if either cast a vote in the June election. If they did, it would have been for an anti-Treaty candidate. Despite the opposition of Cumann na mBan and the split in the IRA on the Treaty, it was overwhelmingly ratified by the Irish people on 16 June 1922. There were 239, 193 votes in favour of pro-Treaty candidates and 133,864 for anti-Treaty candidates; four women anti-Treaty TDs – Countess Markiewicz, Kathleen Clarke, Ada English and Margaret Pearse – all lost their seats. If the election settled the matter of the Treaty, if certainly did not bring peace to the country. Already on 14 April 1922 the anti-Treaty IRA seized control of the Four Courts (which had also been an outpost during the 1916 Rising) and other strong points in the centre of Dublin. On 27 June 1922, under pressure from the British Government to dislodge the anti-Treaty forces there, the new National Army of the Irish Free State began a bombardment of the Four Counts. Thus began the Irish Civil War in which Skinnider and O'Keeffe would both play important roles.

CHAPTER FIVE

Civil War

In March 1922 anti-Treaty forces had taken over the Four Courts in Dublin and called on Cumann na mBan women to join them. Among the IRA leaders in the Four Courts was Liam Mellows whom Skinnider knew from her days in America. Skinnider responded to the call from Mellows and the anti-Treaty IRA, as did many Cumann na mBan women. They supported the garrison by carrying dispatches, transporting weapons and ammunition, and by providing catering and First Aid. In 1916 Skinnider had been part of the militant action in a garrison under fire, during the War of Independence she had served more in a logistics rather than a militant role. Now, as Civil War broke out, she was again central to military action. However, unlike her service in 1916, she would not take up a gun this time, nor would she dress in male attire to fight as a soldier. Her organisational abilities, her co-ordinating skills, and her gun-running expertise were now what was utilised. She was 'in charge of Cumann na mBan operations in Dublin during the attack on the Four Courts, with headquarters at Tara Hall'.[1] She initially stationed herself in Barry's Hotel, off O'Connell Street, where she worked as part of the Quartermaster General (QMG) staff of the anti-Treaty IRA.[2] She set up two HQs, one on the south and one on the north inner city, as she thought she 'would be cut off by the river'.[3] At Tara Hall, a trade union hall, she was joined by many Cumann na mBan women, including Nora Connolly O'Brien and her sister Ina. Here she set up an emergency hospital where 'hundreds of girls came ... reporting for duty'.[4] They commandeered food, beds, medical supplies, and provided First Aid.

When the shelling of the Four Courts began on 27 June, Skinnider continued working in the area. She had somehow acquired a Red Cross ambulance and used it as a cover for her activities; mainly carrying dispatches and transporting arms to where they were needed. When some members of the Anne Devlin Cumann na mBan Branch arrived from Glasgow, with guns and ammunition, she met them with the ambulance. They recalled that she screamed at them 'that volunteers in the Hamman Hotel' on O'Connell Street badly needed ammunition, which she took from them and delivered to the hotel.[5] However the anti-Treaty forces in the Four Courts were outnumbered, and after a week of ferocious fighting, during which the Four Courts went on fire with the loss of hundreds of years of documents on Irish history, the garrison surrendered. Her old friend, Mellows, was arrested, as were the other leaders. The focus now shifted to the east side of O'Connell Street where the Dublin Brigade of the anti-Treaty IRA had set up its HQ. Hamman Hotel was under the command of anti-Treaty leader Cathal Brugha and its garrison included a group of Tipperary men, including Dan O'Keeffe, brother of Nóra, sent up to the city to bolster the anti-Treaty republicans.[6] By 5 July, as the buildings around their holdout were reduced to rubble, these anti-Treaty forces had no choice but to surrender. Brugha emerged from a side lane and was shot by the National Army forces. Badly wounded, he was taken to the Mater Hospital where he died two days later. Dan O'Keeffe was arrested and interned in the Curragh, where he would remain until after the Civil War. Brugha's widow, Caitlín, asked that 'only the women of the Republican movement' form a Guard of Honour at his funeral. Skinnider was one of the women who did this duty.[7]

The fighting then ended in Dublin but it was not the end of the war for Skinnider or O'Keeffe. In Dublin 'with the fall of the Four Courts, the whole of the QMG staff was gone'.[8] Skinnider received a note from Mellows, who was in Mountjoy Jail, informing her 'where things belonging to the Dept., were … [she] had my own keys, and [she] got all the books, etc… needed, belonging to the Dept., and carried on the work that Liam had been doing'.[9] Skinnider was now effectively Paymaster General of the anti-Treaty IRA and would continue doing this work, along with her other Cumann na mBan work, until December 1923. During this period, she worked closely with Austin Stack, who had supported the anti-Treaty IRA, becoming their Director of Finance. As part of her work she 'paid the ASU (Active Service Units), paid the AG's staff, and all the Departments – the Assistant Chief of Staff – that was Ernie O'Malley'.[10] She had a team working with her, including couriers (mostly Cumann na mBan women) working for the different officers, particularly after the Republican Government was set up in October 1922. The members of the Council of that Government included Seán T. O'Kelly, J. J. 'Scelig' O'Kelly, Robert Barton, Mary MacSwiney, Kate O'Callaghan, and Austin Stack as Minister for Finance. It was to Stack that Skinnider reported during her time as Paymaster General and from him that she received large sums of money with which to keep the anti-Treaty side going, including the large sum of 'eight hundred and fifty-eight pounds' on 22 September, 1922.[11]

Skinnider was also involved in activities which were reminiscent of her work with the IRA in Scotland before and during the War of Independence. A letter from the Scottish IRA on 27 February 1923 was concerned that the 'stuff' they had sent with the 'girlys' to Dublin had been delivered to the Grasham [*sic*] [Gresham Hotel].[12] Until January 1923 'stuff' was still being sent to Dundalk and Dublin and was delivered to 'the following; Miss H——ys, Miss D——ly, Miss S———der, Miss O' M——in and Mrs D——ey'.[13] The Miss S———der was Margaret Skinnider, who worked with her Scottish comrades in bringing arms into Ireland until her arrest. Nóra O'Keeffe had also taken an anti-Treaty stance. Nan Walsh (who would later marry Joseph O'Keeffe, a brother of Nóra's) worked with the Cork and Waterford Brigades of the IRA. Taking the anti-Treaty side herself she continued intelligence gathering for the anti-Treaty IRA. Once Civil War broke out she served as 'a guide to [Cumann na mBan] organiser (Miss O'Keeffe) and spent a good deal of time in conveying her from place to place within the Brigade area'.[14] O'Keeffe (Nóra) initially did dispatch work for the anti-Treaty forces in the Cork, Tipperary and Waterford areas, and Nan Walsh took her around the area.[15] Cumann na mBan would again, as it had done in the War of Independence, play an integral role in the dissemination of republican propaganda. Brigid (Bridie) O'Mullane, who ran the publicity office for the anti-Treaty IRA, appointed O'Keeffe as anti-Treaty publicity agent in Tipperary. Because of this O'Keeffe would spend most of the Civil War in Tipperary where she was Director of Publicity for the Third Tipperary Brigade. With Seán Fitzpatrick she edited an anti-Treaty newspaper, *Chun an Lae*, which ran from December 1922 to February 1923.[16] As Séumas Robinson noted of the Third Tipperary Brigade during the Civil War, we 'ran a weekly newspaper, "Chun an Lae", with Nóra O'Keeffe as our Director of Publicity, from a foolproof dugout at Maher's of Blackcastle [Tipperary]'.[17] The notoriety of both Skinnider and O'Keeffe did not pass unnoticed with the Free State authorities. O'Keeffe was arrested in Tipperary in February 1923, imprisoned in Cork Jail, and later transferred to Kilmainham Gaol. Earlier, on 26 December 1922,

Skinnider had been arrested at their home, charged with possession of a revolver, and imprisoned in Mountjoy Gaol. Her friend, Nora Connolly O'Brien, took over her position as Paymaster General of the IRA until she, too, was arrested on 14 January 1923, and also imprisoned.

Over 600 Cumann na mBan women were arrested during the Civil War. The women were initially placed in prisons around the country, including Mountjoy, Cork, and Tullamore Jail, and Tralee Prison. Many of their erstwhile comrades in the National Army, and indeed in the pro-Treaty women's organisation, Cumann na Saoirse, knew of the importance of Cumann na mBan to the continuation of a guerrilla war. They understood that stopping the women would impact adversely on the anti-Treaty IRA. The women's work on intelligence gathering, spying, dispatch carrying, keeping the official work of the army (like the QMG staff) going, delivering arms and ammunition to ambushes, as well as running safe houses, securing provisions for the men, and providing First Aid were all essential to the smooth functioning and well being of the anti-Treaty IRA. While the British Crown Forces had been slow to realise this, the Free State National Army was not. They knew what the women could do, they had worked with them before, and now they had to prevent them from carrying out their activities. In October 1922 Richard Mulcahy, Commander-in-Chief of the National Army, set up military courts. Anyone arrested for an act of war (carrying guns or ammunition) faced imprisonment or a death sentence, while carrying documents relating to activities of the Free State authorities was an act of treason and carried a sentence of imprisonment. Under this Coercion Act those arrested were to be tried by military courts and all responsibility for these military and political prisoners lay with the army. This directly impacted on Cumann na mBan as their main work was dispatch carrying and arms transportation. While the threat of execution was not used against any woman caught with a gun (Skinnider was one of those), it was used against men. For example, Erskine Childers, Chief of Propaganda of the anti-Treaty IRA, who was arrested in possession of a revolver was executed on 24 November 1922. The Government also used execution as a deterrent. The IRA assassinated Seán Hales, a Free State TD, in early December 1922, and in response the Government had four imprisoned republican prisoners – Rory O'Connor, Joseph McKelvey, Dick Barrett, and Skinnider's friend and comrade from her New York days, Liam Mellows, executed.

While the Government did not seriously consider executing any woman arrested for anti-Treaty activities, they did recognise the importance of the women to the propaganda and communication network of the IRA. W. T. Cosgrave, the President of the Executive of the Free State Government, stated that 'the mainstay of trouble that we have had was the activity of women'.[18] Questioned about how a 'war on women', especially as dozens were arrested on seemingly trivial changes, would be received by the Irish public, he responded that it was 'not possible to consider these women as ordinary females'.[19] When Cumann na mBan members were initially arrested they were imprisoned in their home areas, in local prisons. However, these prisons were not suitable for holding large numbers of women. Many only had male warders, to which the women objected strongly. By February all female internees were moved to Dublin and held either in Kilmainham or Mountjoy Gaols. By that stage Skinnider had been in Mountjoy for two months. The women in both prisons organised themselves, retaining the structure of their organisation in the form of prisoner councils. To form these councils:

> the highest ranking Cumann na mBan officers drew up a set of rules
> sand these were read to the prisoners. A Prisoner Council was formed.

Commanding Officers and Quartermasters and Adjutants were appointed ...Tasks of the Quartermaster included the distribution of food, candles, soap and notepaper. An adjutant was in charge of the collection and distribution of post. The highest ranking officers made representations to the Governor.[20]

In Mountjoy overcrowding was a severe problem, and the women protested. Many women there were well known activists, including Nell Humphreys, Bridie O'Mullane, Máire Comerford, Sighle Humphreys, Lily O'Brennan, Dorothy Macardle, and Margaret Buckley. Several of the Anne Devlin Branch of Cumann na mBan were also in Mountjoy. Hannah Duggan, Lizzie Marrin, Mary Nelson, and Mollie Duffy, all well known to their former comrade, Margaret Skinnider, had been arrested and deported from Glasgow to Dublin. By March 1923, Mountjoy was full so Kilmainham Gaol was made ready for female prisoners, and on 6 February, 43 women were transferred from Mountjoy to Kilmainham. Skinnider was not among them, however, although she might have liked to have been, as both Nóra O'Keeffe and Nora Connolly O'Brien were in Kilmainham. In Mountjoy Skinnider settled in for the long haul as she would have had no idea how long she would be kept. While the women tried to keep themselves entertained, there were often tensions between them. In Mountjoy they divided into two camps, the moderates and the extremists. The extremists wanted to keep the war going, even inside prison, and actively engaged in various protests, which usually brought punishments down on all the women. The moderates resented this but most of the women engaged in protest of one form or the other. This ranged from ignoring prison rules and antagonising the wardresses and governor, to destroying prison property and barricading themselves into cells. One of the most dramatic and dangerous methods of protest used by the women was hunger strike.

Hunger strike had a long history during the revolutionary period. For women like Skinnider it was also a familiar weapon as it had been used during the militant suffrage activism of the previous decade. Her suffragette comrades in Glasgow, such as Helen Crawfurd, had used hunger strike as a weapon of protest, as had Hanna Sheehy Skeffington in Dublin. Irish Volunteers released under DORA conditions in 1917, and re-arrested for breaking them, also used hunger strike as a method of protest, in their demands for political prisoner or prisoner of conscience status. In Mountjoy, in September 1917, dozens of imprisoned Irish Volunteers went on hunger strike for political prisoner status, among them Thomas Ashe, the former Commandant of the Ashbourne Garrison during 1916. That hunger strike began on 20 September 1917, and by 23 September, Ashe was force fed. Within two days of force feeding, it was obvious that he was in serious distress and he was removed to the nearby Mater Hospital, where he died. The propaganda coup offered the Irish Volunteers by Ashe's death was similar in scale to that offered by the death of O'Donovan Rossa, the old Fenian who had died in 1915. His funeral, like that of Ashe, was used as an occasion to publicly display support for the republican ideology. Another hunger strike during the War of Independence had led to the death of the Lord Mayor of Cork, Terence MacSwiney, who had been arrested in possession of seditious materials and sentenced to two years in prison in August 1920. He went on hunger strike in protest at his imprisonment, beginning as soon as he arrived at Brixton Prison in England. His long hunger strike (73 days without food) and death on 25 October 1920 was reported around the world and gained considerable sympathy for the republican cause. As a weapon, hunger strike, was however, a dangerous double-edged sword. The hunger striker could die, conversely the death of the hunger striker could cause untold problems for the authorities. This was especially the case when that hunger striker, as in the case of Mary MacSwiney, was the sister of an already martyred republican hunger striker, Terence MacSwiney.

MacSwiney had begun her first hunger strike in Mountjoy on 11 November 1922 and it lasted 24 days, until 27 December, a day after Skinnider arrived in Mountjoy Jail. MacSwiney's hunger strike was used as a major propaganda tool by Cumann na mBan, both inside and outside the prison. During the strike the women prisoners engaged in both violent resistance to the prisoner authorities and in prayerful rituals such as gathering to say the rosary every evening. Outside the prison, Cumann na mBan organised marches, rallies and mass prayer gatherings at the prison gates in solidarity with MacSwiney. The Free State authorities were terrified that there would be another MacSwiney patriot and, so after 24 days, a weak but still alive MacSwiney was released. The success of the MacSwiney hunger strike encouraged the use of this weapon among the imprisoned women. After the overcrowding in Mountjoy had been relieved by the transfer of prisoners to Kilmainham in February 1923, the remaining prisoners demanded the restoration of privileges. When these were not forthcoming, twelve women, among them Margaret Skinnider, went on hunger strike. One of their number, Margaret Buckley, explained why they did this. The hunger strike, she wrote, was the 'only weapon we could wield, and we felt justified in using it'. The women had been deprived of 'common necessities' and they were also demanding political status, 'in that very jail Tom Ashe [had] suffered and died to obtain'.[21] After seven days the strike was called off, and the Governor restored letters and parcels. Skinnider continued her time in Mountjoy until all the women were transferred to the North Dublin Union on 3 May 1923.

Nóra O'Keeffe, who had initially been imprisoned in Cork Jail, had been transferred from there to Kilmainham in early 1923. On

7 April, 1923 it was reported in the republican newspaper, *Irish Nation (Éire)*, that there were 'between 220 and 250 prisoners here [Kilmainham] at present and they are coming in at a steady rate of 4 and 5 a day'.[22] There were also, at that time, 90 women prisoners on hunger strike as their letters and parcels were prohibited. The 'F. S.[Free State] authorities may attempt to represent this as a strike for release; it is not, it is only to have the order revoked'.[23] The article also described the conditions in 'B' wing where many of the incoming women were kept, as appalling; 'there are about 50 sleeping on the floor, with no furniture of any description in their cells ... they are bringing people in day after day without making provision for them ... there is no heat or light on it either.'[24] The hunger strike for restoration of privileges lasted until 29 March, when the authorities restored access to letters and parcels. Like the women in Mountjoy, the Kilmainham prisoners also elected a Prisoners Council, half of whom were members of Cumann na mBan. The Council then selected three officers, Una Gordon, Sighle Bowen and Nora Connolly O'Brien. By April, several of the women were on hunger strike again. Among them was Nell Ryan (sister of Min Ryan – now Mulcahy), who was released on 24 April, in her 34th day of a hunger strike. Like O'Keeffe she had been transferred from down the country, in her case, Wexford, where she had been arrested for anti-Treaty activities. Even though her brother-in-law, General Richard Mulcahy, was Chief-of-Staff of the National Army, she received no privileged treatment. However, as with MacSwiney in Mountjoy, the Free State authorities did not want any woman to die on hunger strike, and between 25 and 27 April 'Nell Ryan and Miss [Annie] O'Neill were released, a few days later Madame [Gonne] MacBride was gone. That same night Kitty Costello was told by the doctor that she was unconditionally released'.[25]

The overcrowding at Kilmainham and Mountjoy continued, however, as more and more women were brought in. The authorities decided to prepare a new location for female prisoners, at the North Dublin Union (NDU), an old workhouse to which women from Mountjoy and Kilmainham were transferred in late April/ early May 1923. All remaining female republican prisoners, in total 51, in Mountjoy, including Skinnider, had been transferred to the NDU by 3 May, while around 200 were to be transferred from Kilmainham. On 30 April, the Kilmainham Governor told the women that the first batch of 80 were to be transferred. At that time, however, Mary MacSwiney, re-arrested and back in jail, and Kathleen O'Callaghan, the former anti-Treaty TD, were on hunger strike there. The rest of the women refused leave while the hunger strike was ongoing, so they holed up on the third balcony of 'A' wing. Their primary demand was that MacSwiney and O'Callaghan be released. Annie O'Farrelly described the reaction of the prison authorities who sent military police to bring the women down and transfer them. The women were attacked, hustled and pushed down the stairs, several lucky to get out 'without a broken head'.[26] O'Farrelly was attacked 'half way down [the stairs] … and … [I] shot into the corridor … I was lifted off my feet and dumped outside in the passage to be searched by Cumann na Saoirse'.[27] The 'girls' she said, were bruised, and some had twisted arms and sprained ankles; she also complained bitterly that the searchers took 'gold bracelets and all kinds of jewellery'.[28]

Once all the women were down from the upper floors, 80 of them were loaded into trucks and transferred to the NDU, with a second batch of 50 women transferred later that night. There were now about 60 women remaining in Kilmainham, among them Nóra O'Keeffe. O'Keeffe would remain in Kilmainham until the late autumn of 1923. Celia Saunders Gallagher, who spent time in

Mountjoy, the NDU and Kilmainham, kept a diary in Kilmainham, in which she mentioned O'Keeffe. On 20 September, the women held a whist drive on 'A' wing and four of the 'B' wing women went across:

> there was a nice crowd and it was a cosy room with a grand fire and I wasn't a bit bored. Nóra O'Keeffe and Effie Taaffe were amongst the entertainers. The former invited me to stay the night but I told her my feet were cold and that I had to do Irish in the morning.[29]

If the remaining women felt that Kilmainham was now 'a more pleasant' place, the women moved from Mountjoy and Kilmainham found settling into the NDU difficult.[30] The Mountjoy women, who had also refused to move to the NDU, had already been beaten up and forcibly dragged to the waiting trucks. There were also undertones of sexual violence in the behaviour of the prison guards and the women in Cumann na Saoirse, bitterly called 'Cumann na Searchers' by their former comrades.[31] In a letter smuggled out from the NDU, after she had arrived there from Mountjoy, Sorcha McDermott reported that, during the battle to get the women there she:

> was assaulted … by four women employed by the Free State. My dress was taken off because I resisted … the prison adjutant, a man of at least six feet of heavy build, knelt on me while the woman assaulted me, beating me about my face and body with my shoes … I fainted … On my recovering consciousness I found myself outside in the passage among drunken soldiers lying in a semi nude state, my clothing saturated with water.[32]

Once the women arrived at the NDU they insisted that there be only 30 women in every cell, with proper beds and bedding. With more women being transferred to the NDU the women already there complained bitterly. As a second batch from Kilmainham arrived 'we put up barricades and refused to allow more than the stated number (thirty) in'.[33] Because of the protest 'the girls [from Kilmainham] had to sleep out in the open'.[34] As with Kilmainham and Mountjoy, a temporary Prisoner Council was convened to discuss and direct the action. The Chairperson was Una Gordon, Council members included Margaret Buckley, Máire Comerford, Sighle Humphreys, Dorothy Macardle, Bridie O'Mullane, Máire Deegan, and, as Director of Training, Margaret Skinnider. The Council decided that until the Governor met them about complaints of overcrowding, the Kilmainham women would have to remain sleeping outside. For over eleven days these women remained camped outside, often in the pouring rain, feeling cold and hungry, until they were eventually allowed in. For their remaining time in prison the NDU was a place of 'discomfort, hunger, cold and dirt'.[35] Tensions over food, parcels, conforming to rules, or demanding political prisoner status, hunger strikes, access to proper bathroom facilities to clean themselves, and demands that they clean their rooms, were among the issues that the Prisoner Council had to deal with. Skinnider's job as Director of Training was to keep the women occupied and fit. She devised wrestling matches and drills like those used by the Cumann na mBan branches she had been in.

Several diaries and memoirs of the time the women spent in prison show that, despite the tensions, the discomfort, the divisions between moderates and radicals, the occasional violence, the hunger strikes, and the politics, the women also created a type of community for themselves. They improvised to make life a little more bearable. In a letter to her mother Annie O'Farrelly describes how the women in the damp, cold and musty NDU, decided by July 1923, that if they were not getting out, then they would make

'winter wear out of [our] blankets. Several blanket coat-frocks have
been captured since we came here and the penalty was stoppage of
letters and parcels for a fortnight.'[36] The Power sisters from Kerry
wrote a memoir of their time in the NDU in which they also
describe the cutting up of blankets to 'make souvenirs of our stay.
These were mostly slippers and small things, but the more
ambitious among us tried larger garments such as skirts'.[37]
Another Kerry prisoner mentions Margaret Skinnider. Hannah
Moynihan reported that on Saturday 9 June, 'Margh S. came to
our dormitory & stayed until 1am'. The women got in a row with
Miss [Josephine] Flood as the Council ordered that there be no
speaking after 11 pm. On 11 June, the women had wrestling
matches and games of rounders – the rounders match was between
'Mountjoy and Kilmainham'. When Mountjoy won, 'we booed
them, and Margt S. threatened revenge':

> she and K Coyle came to our dormitory at 10.30 & we talked and
> argued until 1am. Then on the darkness I struggled to my bed to find
> nothing left but the bare bedstead, so I had to crush in beside M. J.[38]

Skinnider seems to have been a regular visitor to Hannah Moynihan
to chat – Moynihan mentions again on 8 July that she 'got a telling
off from Eithne Coyle for staying chatting with Margt. until 3 am.
Promised to reform'.[39] A photograph of Skinnider taken while she
was in the NDU shows her enjoying the fresh air in the prison yard
while smoking a cigarette. However, she did have her worries;
earlier in July, in a chat with Annie O'Farrelly, she had mentioned
that 'she was very worried about her house as there is no-one
outside to know if it is locked up or not', which of course there
wasn't, as O'Keeffe was also still in prison.[40] Despite all the
attempts to keep themselves occupied and entertained the women

in the NDU were becoming more restless. The Civil War had ended in April 1923, but there was still no sign of their release.

As the summer progressed, the conditions in which the women were living deteriorated. After negotiations with the Governor male prisoners were brought from Arbour Hill Jail to clean out the women's quarters. However, conditions remained difficult and in a report published in the republican newspaper, the *Éire/Irish Nation*, on the NDU, in August 1923, Dr Eleanor Feury wrote that 'scabies and lice were a problems and illnesses like scarlet fever, chickenpox and smallpox were a cause for concern'.[41] As August arrived and there was still no release, a number of women attempted to escape, but failed. As punishment, the Governor stopped all letters and parcels for 21 days, and in retaliation the women refused to turn up to roll call. The situation continued until 21 September, 1923 when General Richard Mulcahy announced that all female prisoners would be released; at that time there were '124 being held in Kilmainham [among them Nóra O'Keeffe] and 199 in the NDU [among them Margaret Skinnider]'.[42] On 29 September, 79 of the Kilmainham women were released and the rest transferred to the NDU. A letter a few days later from Nora Connolly to Hanna Sheehy Skeffington noted that 'Madame Gonne had announced that 75 women were released from Kilmainham and the Union', and she inquired if 'any of our friends were among them? ... Was Margaret or Nóra O'Keeffe?'.[43] And, indeed, O'Keeffe was among the 75 women released.

Skinnider, however, was still in the NDU, along with over 250 women. The war had been over since April, yet new internees were still arriving and others who had been in prison for many months remained incarcerated, with no sign of release. As a protest at their continued incarceration male prisoners around the country began to go on hunger strike. In the NDU, the women, on hearing of the male hunger strikes, held a Council meeting to decide their own course of action. There wasn't consensus on whether a hunger strike was beneficial. Some, like Máire Deegan, felt that a female strike in the NDU would distract from the actions of the men in Mountjoy and that 'few of the girls [are] … fit subjects for a protracted strike of thirty to forty days'.[44] However, on 24 October, 51 of the 84 women in the NDU decided to go on hunger strike. Skinnider had already undertaken three hunger strikes while in prison (one in Mountjoy and two in the NDU), and it seems she did not join this one, although she remained, like the other non-strikers, supportive of the women on strike. However, outside the NDU, support for the hunger strikers was not as it had been when Mary MacSwiney began her first hunger strike in Mountjoy in late 1922, while the prison authorities and the Government were determined not to release the prisoners until the strike was called off. The women not on strike were offered immediate release. Skinnider was one of two women released on 1 November 1923. She went home to join O'Keeffe at their house in Fairview. She had spent almost eleven months in prison.

CHAPTER SIX

Finding a New Sense of Purpose
1924–40

By December 1923 Margaret Skinnider and Nóra O'Keeffe were both back in their home in Fairview. They had spent the previous five years deeply involved with Cumann na mBan and the IRA. Both had also spent most of 1923 in prison. Now the war was over and as they were on the losing side, they had to consider how they were going to pick up the pieces of their lives. Practicalities demanded attention initially. With Cumann na mBan disorganised, and no immediate need for their work as full-time activists, they needed to find jobs and incomes. Skinnider got work as a clerk and bookkeeper for the Workers' Union of Ireland (WUI) in Marlborough Street, founded by James Larkin in 1924. Although a trained and experienced teacher, with her record of anti-Treaty involvement and her prison record, she was not a welcome candidate for any teaching post. O'Keeffe had been a secretary to the Labour leader, Thomas Johnson, and used her typing and stereography skills to pick up some work. She also contributed articles to various newspapers, nationally and internationally, for which she was paid. Their friend and anti-Treaty comrade, Nora Connolly O'Brien, also picked up work as a journalist. Among their close friends in Dublin were Connolly O'Brien and Hanna Sheehy Skeffington, as well as Cumann na mBan colleagues who continued to be involved in the organisation. It was among this close circle of friends and family that the couple looked for support in the immediate aftermath of the Civil War. These women formed a female-centred network of friendship and support for Skinnider and O'Keeffe. There are many letters in the Sheehy Skeffington archives in the National Library of Ireland that show continuous communication between Nora O'Keeffe, Nora Connolly O'Brien, Margaret and Hanna, until Hanna's death in 1946. These letters are at times intimate, revealing the domestic day-to-day life of Skinnider and O'Keeffe, at times gossipy and conversational, at times serious about money (or the lack of same), and, at times, about their continuing activism, particularly their feminist, trade union and female republican activism.

Life was not easy, personally, financially or politically, in those early years of the Irish Free State, particularly for women who had fought for a Republic which had promised to deliver full and equal citizenship for women. The activities of women such as Skinnider and O'Keeffe had been integral to the struggle for Irish independence. However, in the new Irish Free State, their position as women was not 'on an equality with the men' as had been promised in the Proclamation. The new State, governed by the most conservative of revolutionaries, in tandem with the growing influence of the Catholic Church, viewed women primarily as wives and mothers; their contributions would be most acceptable through these roles and in the domestic sphere. Women had been granted full suffrage with men in the 1922 Constitution, however, attempts to gain more equality stalled. From its inception the Cumann na nGaedheal Governments of the 1920s introduced gendered legislation that chipped away at the civil rights of women and promoted the dominant discourse of women in the home. Irishwomen's citizenship soon became, as historian Maryann Valiulis has noted, 'rooted in the private sphere … [and] directly related to motherhood within marriage'.[1] Gendered legislation introduced included the 1925 Civil Service Amendment Act which gave the Government

Margaret Skinnider posing as a Na Fianna boy, c.1915. This photo was used in her book, *Doing My Bit of Ireland* (1917). The image was altered before inclusion in the book. Image courtesy of James Langton.

The original photo of Margaret Skinnider posing as a Na Fianna boy, *c.*1915. Image courtesy of Fergan O'Sullivan.

Margaret Skinnider and Nora Connolly with friends, Cooney Island, New York, USA. May 1918. Image courtesy of Janet Wilkinson.

Margaret Skinnider in the North Dublin Union, 1923. Image courtesy of Fergan O'Sullivan.

Margaret Skinnider and Nóra O'Keeffe at their home in Clontarf, *c.*1930s. Image courtesy of Janet Wilkinson.

Margaret Skinnider and Nóra O'Keeffe at their home in Clontarf, with Frank O'Sullivan (Margaret's nephew) and Tommy Skinnider (Margaret's brother), 1958. Image courtesy of Janet Wilkinson.

Margaret Skinnider, proudly wearing her revolutionary medals, addressing an audience on the 50th anniversary of the Rising, 1966. Image courtesy of Janet Wilkinson.

Margaret Skinnider with past Presidents of the INTO, including three women Presidents, M. Skinnider (second row middle, 1956) with, in the front row, Miss B. Bergin (1950) and Mrs K. M. Clarke (1945). The photograph taken in 1971, shortly before Margaret Skinnider died. Image courtesy of the INTO Archive.

Margaret Skinnider, President of the INTO leaving for Manila, Philippines, 1956. Courtesy of the INTO Archives.

Margaret Skinnider (second from right), her sister Georgina O'Sullivan (Geo), her nephews, Frank and Fergan, and Nora Connolly O'Brien (far right) on holidays in Inishlacken, Connemara, summer 1937. Image courtesy of Janet Wilkinson.

the power to ban women from certain civil service exams; the 1925 Juries Bill which would deny women the right to sit on juries; followed by the 1927 Juries Bill which would allow women to opt out of serving on juries; as well as the 1929 Censorship of Publications Act which banned advertising on contraception.[2]

Representation of women at the centre of Government, in the Dáil, was also inadequate, especially when it came to defending women's rights. The Fourth Dáil, elected on 27 August 1923, included five women TDs: Constance Markievicz, Kathleen Lynn, Caitlín Brugha, Mary MacSwiney, and Margaret Collins-O'Driscoll. However, four of the five, Markievicz, Lynn, Brugha, and MacSwiney, were all anti-Treaty and did not take their seats. That meant, effectively, that only one woman, Collins-O'Driscoll, niece of Michael Collins, sat in the Dáil for the first decade of the Free State.[3] Collins-O'Driscoll was no feminist and generally voted along party lines on women's issues, so no voices were raised in the Dáil as the anti-women pieces of legislation were introduced. For instance, Collins-O'Driscoll supported the 1925 Civil Service Regulation (Amendment) Bill, which limited the ability of women to take the higher Civil Service exams, and which would directly impact Nóra O'Keeffe's Civil Service career, saying that despite 'being canvassed by very influential members of my sex to vote against this Bill', she failed to see how it infringed on women's rights.[4]

There was more of a feminist presence in the Upper House, the Senate. From 1922 to 1936, there were six women Senators, five of whom were active in opposing anti-women legislation.[5] As the misogyny of the Free State became more evident they often 'collaborated with Cumann na mBan women against the threat to equality manifested in the extreme conservatism and anti-women's equality ideologies of the new political masters, in both Cumann na nGaedheal and Fianna Fáil, of the Irish Free State'.[6]

The Senate women opposed the gendered legislation introduced by successive Free State governments, including the 1925 Juries Bill, the 1925 the Civil Service Amendment Act, the 1927 Juries Bill, and the 1929 Censorship of Publications Act.[7] A major aspect of the social conservatism of the Cumann na nGaedheal Government was its attitude to the female worker, which was to remain a contentious issue throughout the 1920s and 1930s, even with the change of Government, to Fianna Fáil, in 1932. One aspect of this concern over the female worker would directly impact on Skinnider's life as a trade union activist. In 1932 a ban on married women working in the civil service and a bar to married women teachers was introduced. The teachers trade union, the Irish National Teachers' Organisation (INTO), of which she was soon to be a member, condemned this move, even as some of its women members voted for the bar, stating that 'a woman's loyalty is to her home'.[8] The reasons cited by the Department of Education for the new marriage bar for women teachers included the fact that 'women could not satisfactorily tend to the duties of both work and home'.[9]

There was also a continuing backlash against the women who had remained in Cumann na mBan, particularly against those women who had been active on the anti-Treaty side. Many, as Margaret Ward wrote, 'had nothing to sustain them but the idealism'.[10] Most found it hard to get work, imprisonment had broken the mental and physical health of many, while others simply dropped by the wayside as disillusionment set in. For those who remained committed the practicalities of earning a living, while continuing their activism, became a priority. While Skinnider and O'Keeffe were able to pick up work, it is obvious that money issues continued to be part of their lives for the next decade or so. In January 1924 O'Keeffe wrote to Hanna Sheehy Skeffington saying that Nora Connolly O'Brien had told her that stenographers were needed for the Táilteann Games. When she [O'Keeffe] had enquired, she had been told otherwise and asked that Sheehy Skeffington 'with your usual kindness, if you can, make an opportunity, see and ask somebody on my behalf'.[11] An undated letter, *c*.1924, again from O'Keeffe to Sheehy Skeffington, celebrates the fact that a 'Mr Raftery' got in touch requesting her to start a job that day, a job she felt would 'pay out fine'. We must, she wrote, 'have a high tea some evening to celebrate'.[12] In July 1924 Skinnider wrote to 'Mrs Skeffington', thanking her from sending a cheque, but returning it as Sheehy Skeffington had neglected to sign it, and writing, 'I don't think the people in the Land Bank would pay me even tho' they do know me pretty well'.[13] This was in relation to a loan Sheehy Skeffington was giving to Skinnider. In 1926, she again wrote, in some distress, to Sheehy Skeffington, as she had been refused a loan from the White Cross to do some building work, and 'everything seems to be going wrong'. She then applied for a loan from another society and used Sheehy Skeffington and Kathleen Clarke as referees.[14] She did get the loan, as O'Keeffe later refers to the fact that family were living in 'Margt's bungalow on this road [Seafield Road, Clontarf]'.[15] In 1931 she wrote to Sheehy Skeffington asking her to be 'a referee once again' for a loan. She was trying to raise money to bring her sister, Georgie, who had married and was living in Australia, home, along with her children as her marriage had failed. 'I thought,' she wrote, 'I was finished with borrowing.'[16] In appreciation for the financial help that Sheehy Skeffington gave the couple, O'Keeffe wrote, in 1933, that she wanted no pay for any typing work she could do for 'Mrs Skeffington' and that 'if and when you can manage to write that life of Francis Sheehy Skeffington, I am entirely at your service'.[17]

Skinnider and O'Keeffe were not the only former revolutionaries who found themselves in dire financial straits in the early years of the Irish Free State. Both pro and anti-Treaty republicans were struggling in a weak economy, so the Free State Government decided to introduce military pensions to help those in need, in particular those who were pro-Treaty. In 1923 an Army Pensions Act was passed which 'awarded pensions for soldiers of the Irish army and revolutionary volunteers wounded between 1916 and 1923'.[18] Then, in 1924, they introduced:

> a series of military service pension acts based solely on the length and nature of service given by those who had fought between 1916 and 1923. Only those who had fought on the pro treaty side for the Free State army in the civil war were entitled to apply for these pensions.[19]

To be eligible for the pension, a person had to have served in one of pre-Truce organisations, such as the Irish Volunteers, or IRA, 1916–21, the Irish Citizen Army, The Hibernian Rifles, Na Fianna, and/or post-1922, in addition to having served in 'the National army or associated security forces, post-1922'.[20] While women had served in the Irish Citizen Army in 1916, the obvious omission from the list was Cumann na mBan, which rendered the majority of women republicans ineligible for the pension. Male eligibility was also limited. Men who had served in the Irish Volunteers/IRA pre-Truce but who had taken the anti-Treaty side, were also refused pensions. There were some women who were pro-Treaty, who could potentially have been eligible. However, only one pro-Treaty woman, former 1916 Cumann na mBan insurgent, Dr Brigid Lyons Thornton, applied. Lyons Thornton had fought in 1916 as a member of Cumann na mBan, stationed with the Four Courts' garrison. She had also been active in Cumann na mBan during the War of Independence, but her eligibility was not based on her membership of any female pro-Treaty organisation; it was based, rather, on her service as an army doctor – she had served in the National Army between 1922 and 1924. On the formation of the

National Army (January 1922) she was invited to join the medical service and, in November 1922, she was given the rank of First Lieutenant. As Kilmainham Jail (where she had spent time as a prisoner after the Rising) filled with anti-Treaty women, she was given responsibility for their medical care.

Lyons Thornton's application was initially rejected. W. T. Cosgrave, the President of the Executive of the Free State, had in the Dáil debates on the Pensions Act stated that women were not eligible. 'The word "person" [on the Act] refers to males', he said.[21] That the Government should be so emphatic in excluding women reflected the general attitude of the authorities to republican women at that time. Cosgrave had been furious at the Cumann na mBan stance on the Treaty, referring to the anti-Treaty women as 'die-hards' whose 'ecstasies at their extremist can find no outlet so satisfying as destruction – sheer destruction'.[22] Those women who had rejected the Treaty were, by 1924, regarded as 'furies', as 'neurotic girls', who had become 'unsexed' and 'unfeminine' in their pursuit of rabid and violent republicanism.[23] Lyons Thornton having been pro-Treaty was no 'fury', even so, her gender posed a problem, which the authorities, and Cosgrave, succeeded in getting around. By 1926, with some pressure from interested parties, the Board of Assessors had reversed their finding and granted her a pension.

Now, however, they were faced with a conundrum as another woman had applied. Skinnider, had also seen service in 1916 (as part of the ICA, an organisation deemed eligible), had been severely wounded in a military action, had also given service during the War of Independence, but, unlike Lyons Thornton, was anti-Treaty. On 27 January 1925 she sent a letter to the Department of Army Pensions, stating her wish to make an application and requesting 'the necessary Official Form of Application'.[24] She applied under the Army Pensions Act, 1923 for the Wound Pension or Gratuity.

Her rank in 1916 was, she wrote, a 'private in the Irish Citizen Army', under the command of 'Commandant James Connolly'. Her wounds, were 'two gunshot wounds in shoulder and one gunshot wound quarter inch from spine, received in action about 2 am, Thursday, April 27th, 1916'.[25] A letter sent from the Office of the Adjutant General to the Department of Defence on 4 March 1925, referenced her application and also noted:

> I would add for your information that the applicant has been a prominent Irregular [anti-Treaty activist] since 1922 and was arrested in possession of a revolver and ammunition on 26th December 1922. She is at present stated to be Chief Officer of the Cumann na mBan.[26]

This application posed a serious problem for the authorities. Skinnider was a relatively well known 1916 insurgent, but she was, and continued to be, a senior member of the anti-Treaty Cumann na mBan. On 4 March 1925 Skinnider wrote again asking about her pension application, as she had heard nothing. However, it was being considered; on 16 February 1925, the Army Finance Officer had written that 'some doubt has arisen as to whether the claim is one which can be considered under the Act'. The preamble to the Act mentioned allowances to 'widows, children and dependants' and therefore 'contemplates that the deceased members shall be of the male sex'. It would, he noted, 'be illogical to include the female sex under the term wounded members ... for the purpose of wounds'.[27] Then on 18 March 1925 the Treasury Solicitor wrote that 'Miss Margaret Skinnider cannot be considered ... under the Act'. The interpretation of the Act meant, he noted, that it is only applicable 'to soldiers as generally understood in the masculine sense'.[28]

Skinnider was appraised of the rejection of her application but did not let the matter lie. After taking legal advice she again wrote to the Army Pensions' Department, stating that rejecting her pension application 'because I was a woman' was wrong, as 'I was a member of the ICA when wounded'.[29] As Cumann na mBan were not included in the Act, she could not claim as a member of the Anne Devlin Branch, however, she had, as she rightfully noted, fought in the Rising while serving as a member of the ICA, who were included in the Act. She got a short reply which referred her back to the letter sent in 1925 which dismissed her claim, because as they again noted, 'soldier' was generally understood in the masculine sense.[30] Skinnider's persistence was a mark of her character as the activist she had been since 1912. Also, as revealed by Bríd Connolly, a member of the Central Branch of Cumann na mBan, who knew her and later used her as a referee for her own pension application, Skinnider had applied as 'an experiment to see if they would give it to her'.[31] The experiment showed that they would not, using her status as a women to legally refuse her. However, as Marie Coleman notes, the fact that Lyons Thornton got the pension 'suggests strongly that gender was the pretext and not the reason for the decision'.[32] This view, that all 'Irregulars' were to be denied pensions, was enforced when some anti-Treaty men, who qualified legislatively, were also denied. This reflected what Cosgrave had stated, that he would 'not pay the pension of any person who has been in arms, or otherwise seriously responsible, in connection with the late outbreak [i.e. the Civil War]'.[33]

As a prominent 'Irregular' and as a Cumann an mBan 'Fury', with her 1916 wounds and her ICA service dismissed, Skinnider was, therefore, doubly disqualified. She would eventually be granted a wounds pension in 1938, when she re-applied under the 1932 Army Pensions Act, which was applied also to 'those who fought on the Republican side in the civil war the same classes of pension as were provided for those who fought during the Black-and-Tan War and during the civil war in the National Army'.[34] She got an annual military service pension, at Grade D (£80 per annum), in 1938, following the extension of these pensions to women. By the time she got the pension, both she and O'Keeffe had more security, financially. O'Keeffe has passed her civil service exams and was now working in a secure and better paid position as a clerk. Skinnider had returned to teaching as a substitute teacher in 1927 at the Sisters of Charity National School on King's Inn Street, in north inner city, Dublin. By 1929, she was working full time in the school and would remain there for the rest of her teaching career.

As well as securing their financial situation, both women were still, and would remain, committed republicans. After they were released from prison in 1923, both remained members of a much reduced and disorganised Cumann na mBan. From 1923–5 Skinnider was on the Executive of Cumann na mBan, and from 1925 into the early 1930s, O'Keeffe was on the Executive. Under the guidance of the Executive, a programme of re-organisation began. At the 1924 Convention, the Director of Training 'read a scheme of organisation', which included lectures (to be held fortnightly on historical, political or economic subjects), a choir was to be formed, First Aid classes were to be organised, branch meetings were to be held monthly, an Officers training class was to start, and Games (camogie and rounders) were to be played within branches and between branches which would allow 'members from all over the country to get to know each other and a spirit of self reliance, comradeship and discipline will be fostered'.[35] Skinnider was still the Director of Training of Cumann na mBan, and, as such, was very much involved in organising these lectures, games, drills, and classes. She was, herself, a committed camogie player, organising and playing with her Cumann na mBan branch. A lot of energy from both women went into the re-organising, along practical and ideological lines. Skinnider, for instance, proposed at the Convention in 1925 that 'no member of Cumann na mBan take the declaration or Oath of Allegiance embodied in political tests in connection with employment'.[36] However, this would not help unemployment among Cumann na mBan members. The plight of unemployed members who had been employed by 'Unionists and Free Staters before their arrest' but who now found their employers would not take them back, was discussed.[37] An economic sub-committee, on which Nóra O'Keeffe was a member, was set up, in November 1924, to look into work schemes that might help members. It secured a small loan from the Republican Reconstruction Committee (RRC) and did attempt, in March 1925, to start a small warehouse business producing knitwear. However, it did not last long, and O'Keeffe told the executive that the warehouse would not survive. It closed in December 1925.

There were also other issues to be dealt with. Recruitment was down; many 'girls' were now joining their local Sinn Féin Cumann rather than local branches of Cumann na mBan. Skinnider felt this was 'demoralising' as Sinn Féin could never be anything 'but a political machine' and was against 'our girls' joining.[38] This would become more of a problem when de Valera split with Sinn Féin and formed Fianna Fáil, particularly after he and Fianna Fáil decided to enter the Dáil. At the 1925 Convention, a resolution was passed that 'demanded that no Republican Teachtaí [TDs] enter the Free State parliament'.[39] The President, Markievicz, was the only member who dissented from this resolution; she was soon to become a founder member of Fianna Fáil. She then informed the delegates that she was resigning as President. An election to replace her had to be held. Mary MacSwiney was nominated but did not want to stand, as it was felt the President needed to be resident in Dublin. Eithne Coyle was asked by the Chairman (MacSwiney) to put forward her name and that she should be 'unanimously asked to fill the office'.[40] However, several members expressed the desire for an election and nominations were taken.

Four women were nominated, Eithne Coyle, Margaret Skinnider, Mary Twamley, and Sighle Humphreys. It came down to two in the final round of voting, Eithne Coyle and Margaret Skinnider. Coyle received 33 votes and Skinnider ten, with Coyle deemed elected the new President of Cumann na mBan. In other voting at that convention, Nóra O'Keeffe was elected onto the Executive.

There were, however, injured feelings over the Presidential election. At a meeting of the Executive held on 17 December 1925, a registration letter from Nóra O'Keeffe was read into the minutes. She wrote that she 'expected idealism in the members of the Executive' but recent actions they had taken were, she considered, 'unjust'.[41] She took exception to the 'manner in which' the election for President was carried out at the convention. She felt that the Chairman (MacSwiney) had played an unjust role in influencing delegates to elect a certain candidate. She was disappointed by the 'failure of the Executive to accept a certain person who she considered processed the qualifications of a perfect member of the Executive'.[42] This person was Skinnider, whom O'Keeffe felt would make an excellent President. The Executive felt that they had acted fairly, and the result stood. They also persuaded O'Keeffe that she had no real reason to resign, and she did remain on as a member of the Executive. Skinnider, although she remained a member of Cumann na mBan, was not on the Executive from 1925.

Skinnider was becoming more involved in politics and trade union activism towards the end of the 1920s. She had always remained close, personally and politically, with Nora Connolly O'Brien, and was part of the short-lived Irish Workers' Party) which Connolly O'Brien had co-founded, with her brother, Roddy, in 1926. Like Markievicz she may have felt it necessary to step back from Cumann na mBan when she joined other political organisations. Unlike Markievicz, and other comrades such as Kathleen Clarke and Hanna Sheehy Skeffington, she felt there was no ideological place for her in Fianna Fáil. In many ways her politics continued to be more in line with the republican socialist politics she first espoused in Glasgow and which she had always admired in James Connolly. In 1919 she had been a member of the committee which tried to set up 'The James Connolly Labour College'. The Socialist Party of Ireland (SPI), of which she was also a member, was instrumental in setting up this College. In the *Watchword of Labour* an appeal for lecturers for the College, advised that a 'working class outlook' was an essential requirement.[43] The 1920 April–May edition of *The Irish Citizen*, bemoaned that fact that not many working-class women were attending the College, especially as there was 'no sex bar in the classes and there were several women on the Management Committee', including Skinnider.[44] Unfortunately, the Labour College never recovered from a raid by the British Military on its building in 1920 and classes ceased.

These activities were an indication that Skinnider's politics continued to be socialist in outlook, and it was among the more left-leaning, socialist and trade union activists that she found her political home. The Irish Workers' Party had several old friends in it, including Maud Gonne MacBride, Charlotte Despard, and Connolly O'Brien. The party, of whose provisional committee she was a member, sought to recruit members of Sinn Féin who were disillusioned by the split, but not inclined to join Fianna Fáil. Among its aims was the:

> establishment of a Workers Republic, based on the Workers' and Farmers' Council; organisation of a Workers' Party, based on recognition of the class struggle; a progressive agrarian policy linking the working farmers with the Labour Movement; a political party that will secure that only actual workers accepting the party's principles will be elected to national and local bodies; and an educational policy aiming at the establishment of a Workers' Labour College.[45]

However, the party soon dissolved (in 1927), after its failure to supplant James Larkin's Irish Worker League, as the Irish affiliate of the Communist International, and Skinnider was once again without a political home.

In October 1927, she managed to get some work as a substitute teacher at the Sisters of Charity National School in King's Inns on Dublin's northside. She had not taught since March 1919, but she was now given six months' work in the school. Finally, she could return to her old occupation. In October 1928, she received a full-time appointment in the school, where she became one of 19 women on the staff. In line with her socialist politics, one of the first things she did was join the teachers' trade union, the Irish National Teachers' Organisation (INTO). Her teaching appointment gave her and O'Keeffe real financial security for the first time in a decade. It also gave her a place, the INTO, in which she would concentrate her activism for the next four decades. She was also still very much involved with Cumann na mBan. A list of 'Women involved with Organisations listed as dangerous by the Free State CID in 1930' included Skinnider as a member of Cumann na mBan and O'Keeffe as a member of Sinn Féin. Remaining a committed republican, she was also one of just 37 women who attended the Cumann na mBan Annual Convention in June 1933.[46] Indeed, into the 1930s, republicans on the run sometimes stayed at her Clontarf house. She also had the sad duty of attending the funerals of several of her old revolutionary comrades, including that of Countess Markievicz in 1927. She, like many members of Cumann na mBan, was dismayed at the proposed new Constitution in 1937, which was, as Kathleen Clarke wrote, 'an attempt to take from women the equal rights and opportunities accorded us in the 1916 Proclamation'.[47] This referred to the articles in the document which positioned women in the home:

41.2.1° In particular, the State recognises that by her life within the home, woman gives to the State a support without which the common good cannot be achieved. 41.2.2° The State shall, therefore, endeavour to ensure that mothers shall not be obliged by economic necessity to engage in labour to the neglect of their duties in the home.

A letter from O'Keeffe to Sheehy Skeffington, also in June 1937, noted that 'Margaret ... was only saying that a good live women's organsation was much needed'.[48] Sheehy Skeffington had denounced the proposed Constitution as contrary to the ideals of the 1916 Proclamation, and said the articles on women were 'fascist proposals, endangering [women's] livelihood, cutting away their rights as human beings'.[49] Women's organisations, including Cumann na mBan, banded together to campaign against these articles, but were ultimately unsuccessful. As a new decade approached Skinnider was well established in her work and in the INTO, but the Irish State, for which she had fought, did not see or treat her, as a woman as 'on an equality with the men'. There were more battles yet to come.

CHAPTER SEVEN

Teacher, Feminist, Politician, Trade Union Activist
1941–72

Skinnider's main activism, for the rest of her working life, was with the INTO. The INTO is one of the oldest trade unions in the country, having been established in 1868, originally as the Irish National Teachers' Association, an amalgamation of several associations which had represented teachers' interests. The immediate context of the founding of the INTO was The Royal Commission of Inquiry into Primary Education in Ireland (the Powis Commission), 1868–70, a committee of enquiry into national education in Ireland. The National School system of education had been in place, in Ireland, from 1831, and a National Board was responsible for the governing of the schools' system. This Board set the rules by which teachers did their job which included accurate record keeping, looking after school supplies, and cleaning and maintenance of their school accommodation. There were also clear rules by which teachers were expected to live by, and they could not be involved in any occupation that might 'impair their usefulness as teachers'.[1] However, pay for teachers was low and some of the duties onerous, so they began to form into associations to campaign for better pay and conditions, these associations eventually amalgamating into the INTO in 1868. The Powis Commission reported in 1870 that 'the progress of the children in the national schools of Ireland is very much less than it ought to be', and that teacher training in Ireland was inadequate. The

INTO also helped professionalise teaching, even as more women were attracted into the profession as better paid opportunities for men opened elsewhere; by 1900, over 50 per cent of national school teachers were women. However, despite the numbers of women in education, while INTO often 'objected to the potential loss of salary, promotion and incremental rights of men teachers ... it made little effort to safeguard the status and promotion prospects of women teachers'.[2] This had a real impact on women workers, as education was one of the few professions into which women could, acceptably, enter.

Skinnider herself had been educated at a teacher training college in Glasgow and now worked at a Catholic-run (Sisters of Charity) national school. While the INTO was set up to represent all its members, it did not, even in 1929, have an exemplary record in representing women. In 1912, it had elected its first female President, Catherine Mahon, herself a suffragist, who had already brought up the issue of equal pay for women teachers in 1906. Mahon was a member of the non-militant suffragist group, the Irish Women's Suffrage and Local Government Association (IWSLGA) which would have informed her campaign for equality of pay for women. In 1906, she attempted to get an equal pay resolution through the INTO's annual Congress. It read:

> that as women teachers have to teach every subject which is compulsory on men teachers, and have in addition to teach needlework three hours in the week, they should receive salaries at least equal to those of men teachers, and we ask the same scale of salaries for all teachers, whether men or women, for the teaching of compulsory subjects of the codes.

She was unable to get Congress to agree that the issue of women teachers' pay was important but was allowed put the proposal to local committees. Most, but not all, local committees supported the resolution, but it would be vital for women to get representation on the National INTO Executive if they were to have real success with the campaign. In 1907 Congress provided two designated seats for women. Mahon continued her work in the INTO and became its President in 1912 and 1913. Despite this early promise, however, the position of women teachers within the Irish educational system, and within the INTO, was certainly not 'on an equality with the men' by the time Skinnider became a member.

In 1916, the position of women in the INTO had been served a body blow when T. J. O'Connell became General Secretary of the organisation and, over the next six years, reorganised and restructured the organisation, removing the designated positions for women on the Executive to the detriment of women teachers' rights. The INTO was not, to that point, a registered trade union, so in 1917, it affiliated with the Irish Congress of Trade Unions (ICTU) and the Labour Party. It adopted a new constitution and took back editorial control of its publication, *The Irish School Weekly* (*ISW*). The new constitution diminished the place of women, however, as it:

> provided for a revamped Central Executive Council (CEC), consisting of the President, Vice-President, the outgoing President, four assistant teachers' representatives and four principal teachers' representatives. The provision whereby two places on the CEC were reserved for women was discontinued.[3]

With the discontinuation of the two designated places the make-up of the CEC was mostly male, even though the majority of teachers were women. This meant that the issues particular to women teachers would not, and did not, receive the attention that they needed or deserved. This became especially obvious in the new Irish Free State, which was not supportive of the idea of the woman worker, particularly the married woman worker. In 1929, just as Skinnider got her first permanent position as a teacher, the first proposals for a bar on married women teachers were mooted by the Department of Education. In October 1931 the Chief Executive Officer of the Department of Education's Primary School Branch argued that 'a marriage bar be introduced on three grounds; it would end an undesirable affluence (local jealousy where a husband and wife both had incomes), it would lead to greater efficiency, and it would end emigration of young (male) teachers.'[4]

On January 1932 the INTO was notified by letter that 'all women national teachers who qualified on or after 1 April, 1932 shall, on marriage, cease to be eligible for recognition in any capacity in a national school'.[5] This, of course, would not directly affect Skinnider as she was not married, but the idea of this unjust rule being imposed on women because of their gender would have enraged her feminist sensibilities. One of the main activities of her time, later, on the CEC was a campaign to overturn this 'Marriage Bar'. In 1932, the membership of the INTO demanded action from the CEC to overturn the ban, but up against the power of the state and the church, they failed to have it overturned. The Marriage Bar was secondary to the INTO campaign against pay cuts, however, as these affected all its members, particularly men. The economy in the 1930s had suffered a series of blows, ranging from the impact of the Great Depression, to the Economic War with Britain, which led to increased emigration, falling population and decreasing pupil numbers. This meant that there were more trained teachers than there were jobs. Pay cuts for all and forced retirement of women teachers at 60 (men retired at 65) were ways in which the Government resolved to deal with the oversupply of teachers. As Niamh Puirséil notes, 'enforced retirement at sixty was a double blow for women' as it deprived them of an extra five years' salary, and also meant that they would not have forty years' service, 'the minimum necessary to be eligible for a full pension'.[6] As Skinnider had entered teaching in Ireland in her 37th year, she would only have had just over 20 years' service if the 60 year enforced retirement age for women remained. Women members were aware that the organisation was not doing its utmost for them, despite the fact that, as one woman wrote to the *ISW*, 'there are 6,360 women members and 4,110 men'.[7]

At the 1942 Congress some women activists did ponder on the fact that if all the women members voted for women, there could be an all-woman CEC instead of the sole woman member.[8] However, the economy was one of the main issues facing all teachers in the late 1930s. In September 1939, war broke out again in Europe, with Britain declaring war on Germany. The Free State remained neutral and a state of emergency was declared. The first cuts to teachers' salaries had been made in 1923, and despite campaigns for pay restoration, this had not happened. With rationing, food and heating materials in short supply and prices soaring, teachers were becoming more and more disgruntled. Their pupils were also suffering; both urban and rural children were living in dire conditions, with too many children turning up to school hungry, which impacted on their ability to concentrate and learn. To add to this, a wage freeze for teachers was introduced in 1941, and even when emergency bonuses were given to teachers in December 1942, a gender gap emerged when men received seven shillings per week while women received only five. The INTO said that the 'size of the award was ... inadequate and they stressed that an increase in the basic scale was 'absolutely essential'.[9] On 2 October 1942 the Dublin City Branch of the INTO, to which Skinnider belonged, demanded 'an immediate increase in the remuneration of teachers commensurate with the great increase in the cost of living'.[10] As anger mounted at the inaction of government, and the inability of the CEC to get any results, all the issues INTO members were dealing with led to mounting frustrations. As the editor of the *ISW* wrote in the May 1944 issue:

> the pity is that the tradition of bad school buildings, underpaid teachers and rigid bureaucratic control is as strong as ever it was and the public have come to regard education, not as something productive and basic, but as a big debt in the National Accounts.

In October 1945 a meeting of Dublin teachers, including Skinnider, at the Mansion House, voted in a secret ballot, 999 votes to 47, to go on strike, when and if instructed to do so by the CEC. The negotiations between the CEC and the government continued to be fruitless, and in December 1945 INTO Gender Secretary, T. J. O'Connell, wrote to the Minister of Education, Thomas Derrig, stating that if the CEC demands on pay scales were not met, the Dublin teachers would go on strike from 17 January. Despite ongoing negotiations no better offer was forthcoming from the Minister, and after several meetings and conferences his unimproved offer was rejected by 4,749 votes to 3,773 votes by the INTO membership. The strike of the Dublin teachers began on 4 March 1946. Minister Derrig criticised the strike as a challenge to the authority of the government and stated that it had been organised as a result of 'the activities of a small but active minority among the teaching body who had agitated amongst the women teachers suggesting to them that they were treated unjustly'.[11]

Despite the condemnation from government the strike held firm. It was co-ordinated by the CEC and the CPC (Central Propaganda Committee), which had been set up in 1945 to pursue all work on the salary campaigns, as well as a dedicated strike committee which had six women members, including two future presidents of the INTO, Brid Bergin and Margaret Skinnider.

This would be Skinnider's first major public action as a member of the INTO. That she was trusted enough to be on the strike committee was a measure of her commitment to, and work in, the INTO, particularly for her local branch, the Dublin City Branch. The strike was to last seven months. The attitude of the Fianna Fáil Government was one of confrontation, with Minister Derrig accusing the teachers of being unreasonable, while the Minister for Finance, Frank Aiken, felt the longer the strike went on, the more money the Government would save on unpaid salaries. When the government then tried to blackmail the INTO by pointing out to parents that it was their children who would suffer from an extended strike, the trade union scoffed at this new-found concern for children as 'when INTO drew public attention some years ago to the mental strain and worry they (the children) were exposed to because of the Department's insistence on outdated teaching methods, its representations were spurned and scoffed at by parents'.[12] Initially, only male teachers were expected to be on the picket line, but soon women teachers, whom it is said showed remarkable enthusiasm for picketing, joined the line too. Support came from many organisations including the Women's Social and Progressive League (WSPL), the Irish Housewives Association (IHA), other trade unions including the Irish Women's Workers' Union (IWWU), and, importantly, they received support from parents' groups. They also drew support from a new political party, Clann na Poblachta, launched on 6 July 1946, in Dublin. With the strike showing no signs of ending, the INTO met for its 78th Congress in April 1946, when about 70,000 children were now out of school. The outgoing President, Mrs K. Clarke, in her address underlined all the reasons why the teachers had no intention of backing down:

> The smouldering resentment of years against stereotyped ideas and bureaucratic administration, the series of harsh enactments against women teachers, and an inspection system which contributes little or

nothing to the value of education – all have helped to fan the flame and have found their fitting climax in the present upheaval.[13]

The strike continued into, and after, the summer holidays. Here was a fight that Skinnider, her Dublin City Branch, and the INTO were determined to see through to the finish. One of their more public actions was to make their way, with banners and placards, onto the pitch at halftime during the 1946 All-Ireland Football Final on 6 October in Croke Park. While the government ministers, and the Taoiseach, sitting in the Hogan Stand, may not have appreciated this demonstration, most of the people in attendance cheered them on. However, this was to be the last major demonstration of the strike. The Fianna Fáil Árd Fheis on 8 October heard Taoiseach Éamon de Valera condemn the continuing strike and appeal 'to teachers to return to work assuring them of a sympathetic hearing should they do so'.[14] Later that month, on 28 October, a Dáil motion recommended that, as the strike was a 'grave source of moral danger and educational loss to the children', the government should set up 'a conciliation committee consisting of representatives of the government, the managers, the teachers and the Dublin School Attendance Committee'.[15] That same day, a letter came to the INTO General Secretary, T. J. O'Connell, from the Archbishop of Dublin, John Charles McQuaid. If the CEC asked him, he wrote, he would write a letter asking the teachers to go back to work. An emergency meeting of the CEC and the strike administrative committee (SAC) was called and it was agreed to ask McQuaid to write the letter, which he did. That evening, the SAC, the other strike committees, and the Dublin City Branch Committee, including Skinnider, were called in and told the strike was off. All teachers were to report for duty to their schools on 31 October.

After seven long months the strike was over. Many members of the strike committee and, more particularly, the Dublin City

Branch, were deeply unhappy with this decision but were unwilling to defy the decision of the CEC and split the INTO. An *Irish Times* editorial is revealing about what it called the 'strange denouement' of the strike, and stated that, in effect, 'the teachers have surrendered'.[16] Anger and hostility towards the government and towards Fianna Fáil, particularly among Dublin teachers, remained a facet of the profession for many years after the strike. While most continued to be members of the INTO, many sought another outlet for their political activities. Clann na Poblachta, which had been founded during the strike, proved very attractive to many disaffected INTO members, including Skinnider. Clann, as it was commonly called, was founded by Seán MacBride, son of Maud Gonne MacBride. The party arose out of resentments at the treatment of republican prisoners, and what it saw as a repudiation of true republicanism by Fianna Fáil. It also reflected the egalitarian roots of Irish republicanism, committed itself to helping the working and labouring classes, to economic and agrarian reform, attacked alleged political corruption, and campaigned on certain specific issues such as the eradication of tuberculosis and a national afforestation project. What the Clann offered was a 'revivalist form of republicanism allied to social reform'.[17] Its founding in 1946 was well timed as a number of issues were creating a backlash against the main parties, Fianna Fáil (who were in government) and Fine Gael, which had been formed in 1933 following the merger of Cumann na nGaedheal, the Centre Party and the National Guard, while the Labour Party was dealing with the fallout from the 'red scare'of the 1940s, and had its own internal difficulties and splits. As a result of internal battles in the Labour Party and the ITGWU between supporters of Jim Larkin and supporters of his main adversary, general secretary of the ITGWU, William O'Brien, the Labour party split, and the ITGWU disaffiliated from it in 1943.

O'Brien claimed it the root of the split was concern over communist infiltration in the Party. Politically it was disastrous for the cause of Labour.

Economically people were struggling in the 1940s, prices were high, wages were static or falling, housing and healthcare were in a dreadful state, there were shortages of necessities like coal, and the Government did not seem to be dealing with the issues. The Lower Prices Council (LPC), formed by the Dublin Trades Council in 1947, was successful in getting thousands of people on the streets. The LPC included representatives from several trade union and feminist organisations including the Women's Social and Progressive League (WSPL), the Irish Housewives Association (IHA), the IWWU, and the INTO. Also represented on the LPC were Clann na Poblachta. As well as campaigning to keep down prices, the LPC recognised the need to highlight women's 'right to participate in the national housekeeping'.[18] The LPC, along with the IHA, decided to convene a 'Women's Parliament', held on 7 October 1947, where over 300 delegates attended. Their programme called for better social and economic conditions for all, school dinners for children, and price controls on basic foodstuffs. At the meeting Skinnider seconded a motion that the government declare a state of emergency, which had been brought about by high prices and use emergency powers to reduce those prices.[19] Large numbers of women activists and teachers now abandoned the more traditional parties and, attracted by the Clann's social reform policies, joined up. Among them were the journalist Maura Laverty and B. Berthon Waters (an economist who wrote for the *Irish Times*) from the IHA, Margaret Skinnider from the INTO, along with three other members of the strike committee. There is no doubt that the teachers were a huge influence on Clann na Poblachta, even if 'the teachers influence over the Clann was always far greater than the

Clann's influence over the teachers'.[20] Both the teachers' strike and the women-led campaign for control of food prices assisted the Clann in mobilising a grassroots movement from its inception.

A general election was called in 1948. Clann had won two by-elections in 1947 so it was ready for a general election. At the 1947 Ard Fheis of the party, Margaret Skinnider had been elected onto the Dublin panel. In joining Clann, she was again following her left-leaning ideals on class and gender rights. She was also joining several comrades from Cumann na mBan and other organisations she had previously been associated with. These included Sighle Humphreys, Kathleen Clarke, Caitlín Brugha, Una C. Stack (widow of Austin Stack), Máire MacSwiney Brugha (niece of Mary MacSwiney), and Kathleen Barry Moloney. Several of the parties in the 1948 election went after the women's vote, but it was Clann, with its emphasis on lowering emigration, and dealing with the high cost of living and high unemployment, that captured much of the politically aware female vote. Skinnider devoted some of her time electioneering and campaigning for Clann candidates. On 10 January 1948 she spoke at a public meeting at Carrickmacross, County Monaghan, in favour of the local Clann candidate, Seán Tully.

Clann na Poblachta won ten seats in the 1948 Election and along with Fine Gael, Labour, National Labour, Clann na Talmhan and independents formed the first coalition, or inter-party govern-ment, with Fine Gael's John A. Costello as Taoiseach. Two Clann TDs were appointed to Ministries – MacBride to External Affairs and Noel Browne to Health. Skinnider remained with the Party, as did many of the women activists. The fact that the inter-party government made improving housing, especially for those living in tenements, healthcare, food subsidies and wages, priorities which reflected the influence women were beginning to have on main-stream politics. Other polices included keeping the price of food down, tackling the tuberculosis crisis, and limiting the number of women emigrating to Britain. Skinnider was appointed to the Clann Ard Chomhairle of Dublin City and County in May 1950, onto a panel of Clann na Poblachta candidates in June 1950, and ran as an unsuccessful candidate for the Clann for a seat on Dublin Corporation, also in 1950. She later reported that her loyalty to the Irish language may have cost her the seat, as she used the Irish version of her name, Maighread Ní Scineadóra, on the ballot, which voters may not have recognised. By 1953 she was on the Party's national executive.

By that time she had also become a senior member of the INTO. In 1949, she had been elected on to the CEC of the organisation. Early in 1949 a representative committee on teachers' salaries was set up under the chairmanship of Judge P. J. Roe (the Roe Commission). It consisted of 18 members, five representing the Department of Education and Finance, six representing the INTO, three managers and one representative each from business, farming and PAYE workers. Skinnider was one of the six INTO members; the report, which was delivered in May 1949, recommended a common pay scale for men and women teachers with a marriage allowance for married men and additional bonuses for those with honours degrees.[21] A report in the *ISW* of October 1949 noted that Bergin (then Vice-President of the INTO) and Skinnider, a signatory to the Roe Report, faced a heavy 'barrage' of questions at a Dublin City Branch meeting. The INTO was not happy with the Government, which was delaying introducing the pay scales, and when they did bring them in, the Minister of Education, Richard Mulcahy, brought them in at a lower rate, although he did concede on a common scale. Some male members of the INTO, especially some single men, were also annoyed that they were now paid the same as single women. Skinnider and the CEC quickly put a stop to these protests. As she noted at a meeting, 'women made up 64 per cent of the membership and single men only ten per cent, but the men were attempting to railroad something which was ... contrary to the INTO's policy of supporting equal pay'.[22]

There was now, also, a renewed attempt, led by the women members, to have the Marriage Bar removed. Several areas of policy drove Skinnider's involvement as a senior member of the INTO, including removal of the Marriage Bar, equal pay for all teachers, university training for all teachers, a common salary scale, and a common retirement policy. In terms of the teaching profession she was herself regarded as an innovative and engaging teacher, and she wished all pupils, including those with physical or intellectual impairments, to have equal access and equal opportunities in schools. She was concerned with the impact that hunger, bad housing conditions, and poverty had on pupils. Delinquency and vandalism, she felt, should concern teachers and parents, and she was always emphatic that parental responsibilities were uppermost; in one speech she said it was time 'we spoke about the rights of teacher and the duties of parents'.[23]

In 1950 Skinnider represented the INTO at the Amsterdam Conference of International Federation of Teachers' Associations. In 1953 she was a member of an INTO delegation which met with the then Minister of Education, Seán Moylan, seeking clarification on teacher salary increases after the budget speech. From what the delegation ascertained, each teacher was to get 'an increase on the first £230 of his or her existing salary scale, with an additional £1 increase for each £22 of existing scale'.[24] Skinnider continued her campaign for pay parity between teachers and in a speech in 1954 condemned the refusal of the government to grant national teachers' pay parity with secondary and vocational teachers. She said that it was dreadful that the men and women 'upon whom 80% of the children of this State depend for their sole education, are less deserving than those who teach the children of a favoured minority'.[25] She continued her work on teachers' salaries and was, in 1955, a member of the Arbitration Board for teachers' salaries. In 1955, she was elected Vice-President of the INTO and in 1956, at the annual Congress, in Bangor, County Down, she was elected as President. She used her incoming speech to speak about pay parity and then moved a resolution calling for:

> salary parity with vocational and secondary teachers, said that this was part of the INTO claim for unity in the teaching profession. Their ideal was an integrated system, all teachers having University training, a, common salary scale and a common system of superannuation.[26]

The Northern Standard in its report on her election mentioned the new President's Monaghan roots, although they claimed, erroneously, she emigrated from Cornnagilta, Tydavet, 'with her parents at a young age'.[27] In July 1956 she left for two months in Manila, Philippines, to represent the INTO at the World Federation of Organisations of the teaching profession. On 23 April 1957 she made her presidential address to the INTO Congress in Killarney. All her ideas about the profession and the role of the teacher were reiterated here. She had long campaigned against vandalism and delinquency and saw teachers as a bulwark against the 'forces at work against the whole Christian way of life'. She also knew that teachers were depressed and stressed by 'low wages, over-crowded classrooms and veiled threats of dismissal … [so] teachers should belong in a profession that must not be controlled by a tyrannical pressure'.[28] They are, she said:

> entitled to their academic freedom, to responsible participation in scholastic efforts, to respect in the community and to remuneration to enable them to maintain standards proper to their position as professional men and women.[29]

The good school, she said, does not have to be a 'palatial building ... but it does mean having thoroughly competent and properly trained teachers with every moral and intellectual qualification for the all-important task of forming the citizens of the nation, and the citizen of heaven'.[30] The speech reflected her dearly held teaching ideologies – proper and equal pay for teachers, proper training and development of teachers, an adequate work environment where teachers could educate the youth of Ireland, for the cause of Ireland.

Skinnider remained, as past President, on the CEC for another year and then, in 1959, stepped down. She had given over 30 years of her life to trade union activism within the INTO. One of her major aims had been achieved in July 1958 when the Marriage Bar for women teachers was finally lifted by the then Minister for Education, Jack Lynch. She also retired from teaching at this time, but she did not retire from activism. In 1960 she was appointed chairman of the Women's Advisory Committee (WAC) set up under the auspices of the Irish Congress of Trade Unions (ICTU). The committee was to advise the Executive Council of ICTU on issues relating to women in the trade union movement. Its role was to further trade union membership among women workers generally, and advise on 'economic, industrial and social matters of special concern to women workers'.[31] Skinnider had begun her activist career as first-wave suffrage activism became militant; she was now ending her career as second-wave feminism was beginning to make its impact felt. While WAC had a torrid time in the beginning trying to get the trade union men to see women's issues and campaigns for equality as important, it would have a major impact in the campaigns for equal pay and equal treatment in the 1970s.

Skinnider would serve as chair of the committee until 1963. At an ICTU conference in Killarney that year, she said that she was anxious to have 'equal pay for equal work' pressed by all union negotiations. The committee had been disappointed that no real effort had yet been put into bringing this principle into 'effect in the civil service or in semi-state organisations, in spite of the fact that the Government has recognised it'.[32] The following year, in a letter to *The Irish Times*, 'Margaret Skinnider, ICA, 1916' wrote an angry letter about the meagre increase given to old-age pensioners in the budget of that year. She wondered was it because pensioners would not march or strike and also if it would not be 'more merciful just to kill them off than to have many of them living in poverty, misery and degradation'.[33] She harked back to the Proclamation of 1916 which promised 'to pursue the happiness and prosperity of the whole nation and all its parts, cherishing all the children of the nation equally'.[34] 'Have the Government forgotten this', she asked, and 'do they realise that but for many of these pensioners they would not be in the positions they now occupy'.[35] At 72 she still had the fire and fury to fight another cause. It is interesting that she signed herself as 'Margaret Skinnider, ICA, 1916', not using her membership of the INTO, or Cumann na mBan, or Clann na Poblachta, to make her point. The ICA was the organisation from which she had fought in 1916, for the ideals contained in the Proclamation. On seeing them neglected, she was, decades later, still fighting for those ideals of full and equal citizenship for all to be realised.

By 1964, she was, however, battling on alone, as her life-long partner and fellow activist, Nóra O'Keeffe, had died in 1961. Margaret and Nóra had lived together for over 40 years in Seafield Road, in Clontarf. Letter, postcards, and photographs in the Skinnider family archive show a full and active life.[36] The couple travelled together, visiting family in Tipperary, in Monaghan and in Glasgow. They often took holidays with friends and family in the west of Ireland, in Connemara, where they rented a cottage. They often visited Monaghan. Nora Connolly O'Brien and her sister, Ina, appear in these holiday photographs, as do several other women friends. They travelled abroad a good deal: there are postcards from Roscoff, Lisieux, and several parts of France in the family archive. They also visited England and Scotland; families histories indicate both women had a love of travel. Both were also very close to their families and had, at times, Skinnider or O'Keeffe family staying with them. Both also had family living nearby: Thomas Skinnider and Georgie O'Sullivan (née Skinnider) lived in Dublin from the 1930s on, and Brigid O'Dwyer (née O'Keeffe) lived in Fairview. Skinnider had an interest in wolfhounds, several appear in the photographs and she bred and showed them, with some success, in competitions. O'Keeffe had an interest in history, legend and local lore and published folk stories in national and local newspapers, usually under her Irish name, Nóra Ní Chaoimh. They attended funerals of old comrades together and attended several State occasions; in 1949 they are both listed as guests at ceremonies to mark the coming into operation of the Republic of Ireland Act. Both had very full public lives, and their private life would have been a space of togetherness, comfort and relaxation to them.

Sadly, Nóra O'Keefe died in August 1961, aged 72, of cardiac failure. Her obituary refers to her membership of Cumann na mBan and her association with the Third Tipperary Brigade of the IRA. It mentioned that she was in Cork and Kilmainham Jail in 1923 because of her anti-Treaty activities. She was survived, it noted, by her brother, Mr Con O'Keeffe of Glenough, and her sister Mrs O'Dwyer of Fairview and another sister, Sr Mary Benedict of Redhill, Surrey.[37] There was no mention of Margaret Skinnider, her partner of over 40 years. O'Keeffe was taken home to Tipperary and buried in Kilnatrick Cemetery, Dundrum. For the following ten years Margaret Skinnider put a memorial in the *Irish Independent* on O'Keeffe's anniversary. It read, on each anniversary: 'in loving memory of my dear friend, Nóra O'Keeffe, late of 134 Seafield Rd., Clontarf, who died Aug. 12, 1961. Sacred Heart of Jesus Grant her eternal rest. Mass offered – Margaret.'[38] Skinnider herself died just over ten years after O'Keeffe. By 1971 she was living at Sion Road in Killiney, County Dublin. She died on 11 October 1971, after several weeks as a patient in St Michael's Hospital in Dún Laoghaire. On her death all the newspapers mentioned her birth in Glasgow, her connection with Monaghan, that she was a former President of the INTO, and had 'fought in the College of Surgeons under Countess Markievicz in 1916 and throughout the War of Independence. She was wounded twice'.[39] In fact, she was wounded three times and survived 55 years after receiving those wounds. A requiem mass, at which the President and the Taoiseach were represented, was held at the Church of Our Lady of Victories, Sallynoggin, County Dublin. Some old comrades from the ICA, the old IRA and Cumann na mBan, as well as colleagues from Clann na Poblachta and the INTO, were also at the mass. Afterwards her remains were taken to Glasnevin Cemetery where she was buried, with full honours, in the republican plot beside her old friend and revolutionary comrade, Countess Markievicz.

Conclusion

According to Cumann na mBan member, Eithne Coyle, it was 'a curious fact that women as women got a very meagre place in the pages of history. And Irish history, I am sorry to say, is no exception to the rule.'[1] After the foundation of the Irish Free State, the role that Cumann na mBan and the women in the ICA played in the revolutionary wars was often downplayed, marginalised or overlooked. For most historians, the actions and contributions of men and the roles they played in the transformation of Ireland from a small, neglected, poor part of the United Kingdom to a self-governing state (albeit without the six counties of Northern Ireland) were central. Within the histories of the revolutionary decade from 1912–23, militancy, patriotism and masculinity were deeply interwoven. Women, if they were acknowledged at all, were simply bit players, there to help, not to lead and certainly not as combatants. The fact that republican women had also been implacably opposed to the foundation of the Irish Free State served to further side-line their contributions to the shaping of modern Ireland. Suffrage activism, female nationalism and trade union activism were often simply a footnote in histories of war, revolution, politics, class, and labour. Their names, their activism, and their contributions slipped out of common knowledge. Occasionally they were central to a history book, as in R. M. Fox's *Rebel Irishwomen*, published in 1935, but for the wider readership of mainstream history books, revolutionary women were too often a footnote if acknowledged at all.

As the decades wore on more scholarship was undertaken on the women, beginning with Margaret Ward's invaluable *Unmanageable Revolutionaries* (1984). Since then, over 40 years of research and writing on women and the revolutionary era (1900–23), mainly by women historians and researchers, has led to a real richness of scholarship. In January 2014 the first tranche of the digitised military pensions application files was released. The Bureau of Military History (BMH) witness statements, taken in the 1950s from surviving revolutionary participants, were digitised and released in 2003. Almost 1,770 BMH statements were collected from members of the Irish Volunteers, the ICA, the IRB, Sinn Féin, and, of course, from Cumann na mBan. However, women's contributions comprised less than 10 per cent of the witness statements, reflecting, as Fearghal McGarry notes, 'contemporary assumptions about the relative importance of their contribution'.[2] In the military pension applications hundreds of women, whose stories had previously been known only to themselves and perhaps their families, applied for military pensions. Examination of the women's witness statements and pension applications shone a new and fascinating light on the breath of women's involvement in revolutionary activities. Using these sources, and combining them with other archival materials, memoirs, oral histories, and newspaper reports, historians could now begin to access how integral the women were to militancy, to combat, and to the work of the revolution.

Among the 3,000 pension applications released in the first tranche in 2014 was that of Margaret Skinnider, including both her failed application in 1925 and her later successful 1937 application. The media had the first look at the digitised archive, and most headlines focused on the 1916 woman who had been denied a pension because of her gender. 'Rebel denied a pension because she was a woman', read the headline:

> A woman wounded while fighting with the rebels in 1916 who was refused a pension because of her gender is among the many fascinating stories to emerge from the Military Pensions Archive that has just opened to the public.[3]

And so, Margaret Skinnider re-entered the consciousness of the Irish public. From 2014 on, her story became a mainstay to the centenary commemorations of the 1916 Rising. In several documentaries, exhibitions and books produced specifically for 2016, Skinnider's Easter Rising story was central. The 2016 RTÉ documentary, *Seven Women*, narrated by Fiona Shaw, explored the roles played by seven women in the Rising: Countess Constance Markievicz, Margaret Skinnider, Helena Molony, Louise Gavan Duffy, Leslie Price, Aoife deBurca, and Elise Mahaffy. *1916: Portraits and Lives* was published by the Royal Irish Academy (RIA) in 2016, with drawings by David Rooney of the selected protagonists, including Skinnider. She was selected, as it was noted in a newspaper review, 'as the most seriously wounded of the female rebels, [and who] boasted that she could pass for a boy 'even if it came to wrestling or whistling''.[4] The portrait of Skinnider from the RIA book, as a dispatch rider, dressed in her grey dress and wheeling her bicycle, was featured on buses and public platforms around the country. She was also a central figure in the RCSI 2016 centenary exhibition, 'Surgeons and Insurgents', which ran in the RCSI main College Hall in April 2016.[5] The College Hall was, of course, the space in which she had been operated on by the First Aid women after she was wounded.

In Monaghan, home of her father, and in Scotland where she grew up, Skinnider was also commemorated. The Margaret

Skinnider Appreciation Society in Monaghan succeeded in having a roundabout in the town named after her, the Timpeallán Mhaighréad í Scineadóra (the Margaret Skinnider Roundabout).[6] In Scotland, lectures by Kirsty Lusk and Stephen Coyle reintroduced her and many of the Irish-Scottish participants in 1916 to a new audience.[7] The INTO also commemorated its former President. At the 2016 Congress a talk by Niamh Puirséil, author of *Kindling the Flame: 150 Years of the Irish National Teachers' Organisation*, brought Skinnider back onto an INTO platform. Puirséil detailed Skinnider's involvement in the Rising, but also spoke about her subsequent work as a propagandist, her activism in the War of Independence, her anti-Treaty stance, her life as a teacher, and her work as a trade union activist with the INTO. She introduced Skinnider's words, on her retirement, to the gathered teachers. On that occasion, Skinnider had said all she had done for teachers was done for the good of the organisation, 'it was the organisation that counted, not the individual – the good of the organisation, the good of the teacher and the welfare of children'.[8] She was a woman who 'had done her bit for Ireland' said Puirséil, but she did not stop there, 'the education of children and the welfare of the teaching profession were really her life's work.'[9]

An INTO colleague at the 2016 Congress who had known her said she, being 'a modest woman', had never mentioned her involvement in the Rising.[10] But Skinnider had shared the story of her part in the Rising many times before her death. In 1966, at the INTO Congress, on the 50th anniversary of the Rising, she had 'delighted all with her nostalgic reminiscences of those awesome times'.[11] Ten years earlier, in April 1955, in a commemorative programme for children, devised by Piaras Béaslaí, she was one of six people 'who took part in Easter Week, 1916, to tell of the things they saw and the things they did'.[12] Her talk was a condensed version of *Doing My Bit for Ireland*. She ended by saying, 'as you know, children, we did not win a military victory in 1916 but we roused the people … to join the fight for Independence and rid at least part of the country of the foreign army that had held us in bondage for hundreds of years'.[13] Between 1940 and her death she was interviewed several time by Rádio Éireann about her involvement in 1916, interviews which remain in the RTÉ archives. In 2016 her 1955 interview was reissued on the *Stories From 1916* podcast.[14] Her distinctive Scottish accent can still be discerned, as she recounted the details, as she had written them in *Doing My Bit*.

Skinnider's story had never actually been completely forgotten; aspects of it were always part of the 1916 narrative, particularly her masquerade as a Fianna boy and the fact that she had been wounded. Like Markievicz, another outlier in terms of gender performance and militancy, Skinnider was the sniper girl who nearly died for Ireland. Her subsequent career as Cumann na mBan propagandist, fund-raiser, and dispatch carrier was more invisible in terms of non-normative gender performance, and therefore her activities between 1919 and 1922 were less remarkable. She was simply one of the 'girls' who worked with the men. Her anti-Treaty stance also served to position her as one of the untrustworthy 'furies' in the new State. Like many of her comrades in Cumann na mBan her politics progressed in the 1920s and 1930s, and she devoted her energies to making the new Ireland a place for women and for workers. Many of these former revolutionary women continued doing their bit, and often supported each other. With Sheehy Skeffington, Connolly O'Brien, and other Cumann na mBan and later INTO women colleagues, she was part of a female network of supportive activist women.

One aspect of her life which did remain hidden, certainly to the broader public, was her relationship with Nóra O'Keeffe. It is clear from archival material, that her friends, Sheehy Skeffington and

Connolly O'Brien among them, regarded Margaret and Nóra as a couple. In letters to and from the women, one was rarely mentioned without the other. It is perhaps only now possible to discuss this hidden aspect of her life, an aspect she and O'Keeffe had in common with several other female same-sex couples of the revolutionary period. These include several women known to Skinnider, among them Kathleen Lynn and Madeleine ffrench-Mullen (who organised the First Aid women who saved her in the RCSI in 1916), Helena Molony, Elizabeth O'Farrell (the 'pale girl' who delivered the surrender message to the RCSI) and her partner, Julia Grenan. She also would have known Eva Gore Booth, sister of Countess Markievicz and her partner, Esther Roper. The importance of biographical research in uncovering not just the activist and public lives of these revolutionary women, but also their private lives and choices, is central to a reassessment of the lives and times of these women.

Margaret Skinnider's long life spanned the years that separated first-wave and second-wave feminism. She began as a militant suffragette in Glasgow in 1912 and remained a feminist to the end. In 1963, when the slow progress towards equal pay was causing disappointment among women workers, she recommended that women should 'organise strongly' to overcome the 'prejudice, convention and sectional privilege' they faced.[15] Never one to be stopped by prejudice or convention, Skinnider spent her life fighting, in a myriad of ways, for equality for women, for the rights of workers and for the cause of Irish freedom. As this biography has demonstrated, Skinnider more than did her bit for Ireland.

Notes

Introduction

1   Helena Molony Military Pension Application, MSP34REF11739, Letter, November 1936.
2   Helena Molony to Seán Ó Faoláin, 6 September 1934, Bureau of Military History (BMH), Witness Statement (WS) 391, Helena Molony.
3   Ibid.
4   Ibid.
5   Helena Molony Military Pension Application, MSP34REF11739, Letter, July 1936.
6   Helena Molony, 'Women of the Rising', Radio Telefis Éireann interview, 16 Apr. 1963, RTÉ Sound Archive, Dublin.
7   Ibid.
8   Margaret Skinnider, *Doing My Bit for Ireland: A First-Hand Account of the Easter Rising*, with an Introduction by Kirsty Lusk (Edinburgh, 2016).
9   Ibid., p. 55.
10   Ibid., p. 36.
11   Ibid, p. 56. As her intended audience for *Doing My Bit for Ireland* was American, especially Irish Americans, she referenced the dollar.
12   Ibid., p. 57.
13   Ibid., p. 156.
14   Treasury Solicitor to Army Finance Officer, 18 Mar. 1925, Military Service Pension Collection, MSPC, W1P724.
15   *Irish Citizen*, 27 Sept. 1913.
16   Sikata Banerjee, *Muscular Nationalism: Gender, Violence, and Empire in India and Ireland, 1914–2004* (New York, 2012), p. 91.

Chapter 1

1   Margaret Skinnider, *Doing My Bit for Ireland: A First-Hand Account of the Easter Rising*, with an Introduction by Kirsty Lusk (Edinburgh, 2016), p. 43.
2   Theo McMahon 'The Rose Estate Tydavnet, County Monaghan', in *Clogher Record*, vol. 18:2 (2004), pp 218–56.
3   The Schools' Collection, vol. 0957, p. 137, National Folklore Collection, UCD.

4   Terence McBride, 'Irishness in Glasgow, 1863–70', in *Historical Studies in Ethnicity, Migration and Diaspora*, vol. 24:1 (2006), p. 2.

5   Ibid., pp 2–3.

6   Thank you to Stephen Coyle for the information on the Fenians in Coatbridge.

7   *Glasgow Herald*, 21 Feb. 1882, quoted in William Kenefick *Red Scotland!:The Rise and Fall of the Radical Left, c. 1872 to 1932*, (Edinburgh, 2007), p. 17.

8   *Glasgow Examiner*, 14 June 1902, quoted in Kenefick, p. 17

9   Skinnider, *Doing My Bit for Ireland*, p. 44. The impact of the Gaelic League on Skinnider is evident in her life-long use of her name in Irish, Maighread Ní Scineadora.

10   Information on her Glasgow teaching career from the private archives of Margaret Skinnider's grandniece, Janet Wilkinson, of Perth, Australia. Used with permission.

11   Ibid.

12   Gemma Elliott, '"Women who dared to ask for the vote"'; The missing memoirs of the Scottish Suffragettes', in *Women's Writing*, 25: 3 (2018), p. 320.

13   Laura Schwartz, *Feminism and the Servant Problem Class and Domestic Labour in the Women's Suffrage Movement* (Cambridge, 2019), p. 86.

14   Helen Corr, 'Crawfurd, Helen (1877–1954)', *Oxford Dictionary of National Biography*, Oxford University Press, Sept. 2004; online edn, May 2006.

15   Helen Crawfurd unpublished diary. https://issuu.com/marxmemoriallibrary/docs/helen_crawfurd (accessed 07/12/2018), p. 86.

16   Ibid., p. 89.

17   Elliott, 'Women who dared to ask for the vote', pp 320–1.

18   Ibid., p. 96.

19   In 1913 the British Government sought to deal with the issue of imprisoned, hunger striking suffragettes with the 1913 Prisoners (Temporary Discharge for Ill-Health) Act, commonly known as the Cat and Mouse Act. This Act allowed for the early release of prisoners weakened by hunger strike, once their health had recovered, they could be recalled to prison and the whole process would begin again.

20   Ibid., p. 123.

21   Crawfurd unpublished diary, p. 106.

22   *Votes for Women*, Oct. 29 (1915), p. 34.

23   Ibid.

24   Crawfurd helped establish the Glasgow Women's Housing Association, to combat the war time profiteering by Glasgow landlords, who increased rents on the outbreak of war.

25   Marnie Hay, 'The foundation and development of Na Fianna Éireann, 1909–16', in *Irish Historical Studies*, vol. xxxvi, no. 141 (May 2008), p. 54.

26   Séumas Robinson would take part in the 1916 Rising, Eamonn Mooney did not participate and Joe Robinson and Seamus Reader were incarcerated in Edinburgh Castle at the time and so could not participate.

27   Daniel Branniff, BMH WS 222, p. 3.

28   Skinnider, *Doing My Bit for Ireland*, p. 44.

29 Ibid., p. 44.

30 Crawfurd unpublished diary, p. 118.

31 Ibid., p. 123.

32 Émilie Berthillot 'Smuggling weapons, republicans and spies across the Irish Sea and North Channel (1912–1923): Gaelic friends or foes', in *Études Écossaises* (2018), p. 10.

33 Robinson, BMH WS 156, p. 5.

34 Kirsty Lusk 'Short skirts, strong boots and a revolver: Scotland and the Women of 1916', in Kirsty Lusk and Willy Maley (eds), *Scotland and the Easter Rising* (Edinburgh, 2016), p. 124.

35 Seamus Reader, BMH WS 627, p. 6.

36 Letters in Private Collection of Rosemary Mahoney. This letter was to John O'Donnell, written by Skinnider in March 1917, from Boston.

37 Skinnider, *Doing My Bit for Ireland*, p. 45.

38 Lusk, 'Short skirts, strong boots and a revolver', p. 126.

39 Skinnider, *Doing My Bit for Ireland*, p. 45.

40 Ibid., p. 43.

Chapter 2

1 Margaret Skinnider, *Doing My Bit for Ireland: A First-Hand Account of the Easter Rising*, with an Introduction by Kirsty Lusk (Edinburgh, 2016), p. 45.

2 Ibid.

3 Ibid., p. 50.

4 Lisa Weihman, 'Doing my bit for Ireland: Transgressing gender in the Easter Rising', in *Éire-Ireland*, vol. 39:3 & 4 (Fall/Winter, 2004), p. 232.

5 Ibid., p. 233.

6 Skinnider, *Doing My Bit for Ireland*, p. 60.

7 Ibid., p. 61.

8 Ibid., p. 62.

9 Ibid., p. 71.

10 Ibid.

11 Ibid., p. 73.

12 Mary McAuliffe, 'Kerry and the Irish Volunteers 1913–1917', in Bridget McAuliffe, Mary McAuliffe, Owen O'Shea (eds), *Kerry 1916: Histories and Legacies of the Easter Rising* (Kerry, 2016), p. 62.

13 Skinnider, *Doing My Bit for Ireland*, p. 85.

14 Volunteers and Cumann na mBan also rose in Enniscorthy, County Wexford, Ashbourne, County Meath, and Athenry, County Galway.

15 Rosemary Cullen Owens, *A Social History of Women in Ireland, 1870–1970: An Exploration of the Changing Role and Status of Women in Irish Society* (Dublin, 2005).

16 McAuliffe 'From Inghinidhe na hÉireann to the Irish Citizen Army: Women, radical politics & the 1916 Rising', in *Saothar: The Journal of the Irish Labour History Society* Issue 41 (2016), p. 74.

17 Helena Molony, BMH WS 391, p. 30.

18 Rosanna Hackett, BMH WS 546, p. 4.
19 Ibid., p. 3.
20 Skinnider, *Doing My Bit for Ireland*, p. 89.
21 Ibid., p. 90.
22 Ibid.
23 Derek Molyneux and Darren Kelly (eds), *When the Clock Struck in 1916: Close Quarter Combat in the Easter Rising* (Cork, 2015), p. 62. As well as the men and women of the ICA Mallin also had some Irish Volunteers and Cumann na mBan women under his command.
24 Fearghal McGarry, *The Rising, Ireland: Easter 1916* (Oxford, 2010), p. 131.
25 Skinnider, *Doing My Bit for Ireland*, p. 101.
26 Ibid., p. 120.
27 Ibid., p. 107.
28 Ibid., p. 120.
29 Ibid., p. 108.
30 Ibid.
31 Ibid., p. 116.
32 Ibid.
33 Ibid.
34 Ibid., p. 117.
35 Ibid., p. 116.
36 Weihman, 'Doing my bit for Ireland', p. 235.
37 Mary McAuliffe and Liz Gillis, *We Were There: 77 Women of the Easter Rising* (Dublin, 2016), p. 78.
38 Ibid., pp 119–20.
39 Margaret Skinnider, Military Pension Application File, MSP34REF19910.
40 Ibid.
41 Frank Robbins, *Under The Starry Plough: Recollections of the Irish Citizen Army* (Dublin, 1977), pp 116–17.
42 Ibid., p. 120.
43 Rosanna Hackett, Bureau of Military History, Witness Statement, BMH WS 546, p. 8.
44 Skinnider, *Doing My Bit for Ireland*, p. 124. The 'pale and scared girl' was Cumann na mBan member and rebel, Elizabeth O'Farrell, who brought the surrender notifications from Pearse and Connolly to all the insurgent garrisons.

Chapter 3

1 Margaret Skinnider, *Doing My Bit for Ireland: A First-Hand Account of the Easter Rising*, with an Introduction by Kirsty Lusk (Edinburgh, 2016), p. 127.
2 Reference Letter from Nora Connolly O'Brien in Margaret Skinnider's Military Pension Application File, MSP34REF19910.
3 Skinnider, *Doing My Bit for Ireland*, p. 143.
4 Ibid.
5 Ibid., pp 149–50.

6 Ibid., p. 152.

7 Frank Robbins, *Under The Starry Plough: Recollections of the Irish Citizen Army* (Dublin, 1977), pp 155–6.

8 Ibid.

9 Margaret Ward, *Hanna Sheehy Skeffington: A Life* (Dublin, 1997), p. 18.

10 Ibid., *Unmanageable Revolutionaries: Women and Irish Nationalism* (Dublin, 1983), p. 118.

11 These bodies would soon amalgamate to form the Irish National Aid Association and Volunteer Dependents Fund (INAAVDF). See Senia Pašeta, *Irish Nationalist Women, 1900–1918* (Cambridge, 2013), pp 201–11.

12 Skinnider, *Doing my Bit for Ireland*, p. 130.

13 The *Catholic Bulletin* was first published in 1911 as *The Catholic Book Bulletin: A Monthly Review of Catholic Literature*. It was a family magazine with popular appeal and an estimated circulation of 10–15,000. One of the few magazines to escape censorship after the Rising, between May and December 1916, articles sympathetic to the nationalist cause appeared often.

14 Áine Ceannt was the widow of Éamon Ceannt, Muriel McDonagh was the widow of Thomas McDonagh, Lillie Connolly was the widow of James Connolly, Agnes Mallin was the widow of Michael Mallin (Commandant in the RCSI) and Kathleen Clarke was the widow of Tom Clake; all the men had been signatories to the 1916 Proclamation. Nannie O'Rahilly was the widow of Michael, 'The' O'Rahilly, who was killed on Moore Street during the withdrawl from the GPO. Hanna Sheehy Skeffington was the widow of Francis, who had been wrongfully executed by British troops at Portobello Barracks during the Rising.

15 Clair Wills, *Dublin 1916; The Siege of the GPO* (London, 2009), pp 110–16.

16 Ibid.

17 Damien Murray, *Irish Nationalists in Boston: Catholicism and Conflict, 1900–1928* (Washington, 2018), p. 213.

18 Margaret Ward, *Hanna Sheehy Skeffington: Suffragette and Sinn Féiner; Her Memoirs and Political Writings* (Dublin, 2017), p. 143.

19 Margaret Skinnider Military Pension Application File, MSP34REF19910.

20 Robbins, *Under The Starry Plough*, pp 156–8.

21 Nora Connolly O'Brien in Uinseann Mac Eoin, *Survivors: The Story of Ireland's Struggle* (Dublin, 1980), p. 206.

22 Ibid.

23 Ibid.

24 Ibid.

25 *The Gaelic American*, vol. xv, no. 6 (9 Feb. 1918), p. 7.

26 Ward, *Hanna Sheehy Skeffington*, p. 201.

27 Robbins, *Under The Starry Plough*, p. 181.

28 Joanne Mooney Eichacker, *Irish Republican Women In America-Lecture Tours, 1916–1925* (Dublin, 2003), p. 88.

29 Ibid.

30 Letters in Private Collection of Rosemary Mahoney. This letter was to Julia Fraher Rohan, written by Skinnider in September 1917, from Brooklyn. Julia Fraher Rohan had emigrated with her five sisters to Boston from

Ballylanders, County Limerick. She was a member of Cumann na mBan and very involved in fundraising in America. Nora Connolly and Margaret Skinnider were visitors to and friends with Fraher Rohan in Boston during 1917–18. She was also in communication with Min Ryan.

31 Eichacker, *Irish Republican Women*, pp 90–1.

32 Ward, *Suffragette and Sinn Féiner*, p. 146.

33 An original handwritten manuscript of *Doing My Bit for Ireland* is in the Burns Library, Boston College. Loretta Clarke Murray Collection – Women in Revolutionary Ireland, MS2060_016, Box 4, Journal of 1916. There are some differences between the handwritten draft and the published version, it is obvious that an editorial hand shortened the published version. However, the details of events and people remain similar.

34 Letters in Private Collection of Rosemary Mahoney. This letter was to John O'Donnell, written by Skinnider in March 1917, from Boston.

35 Liam Harte (ed.), *A History of Irish Autobiography* (Cambridge, 2018), p. 113.

36 Skinnider, *Doing My Bit for Ireland*, p. 104.

37 Karen Steele 'When female activists say "I"', in Gillian McIntosh and Diane Urquart, *Irish Women at War in the Twentieth Century* (Dublin, 2010), p. 61.

38 Skinnider, *Doing My Bit for Ireland*, pp 130–2.

39 Lisa Weihman, 'Doing my bit for Ireland: Transgressing gender in the Easter Rising', in *Éire-Ireland*, vol. 39: 3 & 4 (Fall/Winter, 2004), p. 245.

40 Ibid.

41 Ibid., p. 244.

42 Ibid., p. 245.

43 *The Detroit Times* (6 July 1917), p. 6.

44 Dorothy Day, 'The book of the month'. A review of *Doing My Bit for Ireland* by Margaret Skinnider, in *Masses*, Aug. 1917, pp 37–8.

45 Letters in Private Collection of Rosemary Mahoney.

46 Dear Julia: Personal Reflections on 1916 and its Aftermath https://irishamerica.com/2016/03/dear-julia-personal-peflections-on-1916-and-its-aftermath/ accessed 02/04/2019.

47 *The Gaelic American*, vol. xv:28 (13 July 1918).

48 'Dear Julia: Personal reflections on 1916 and its aftermath'https://irishamerica.com/2016/03/dear-julia-personal-peflections-on-1916-and-its-aftermath/ accessed 02/04/2019.

49 Ward, *Suffragette and Sinn Féiner*, p. 18.

50 Eichacker, *Irish Republican Women*, pp 90–1.

51 Ward, *Suffragette and Sinn Féiner*, p. 19.

52 Ibid.

53 PRO London, CO (Colonial Office Papers for Ireland) 904/215-203, RIC Police Report, 10 July 1918.

54 Connolly O'Brien in Mac Eoin, *Survivors*, p. 207.

55 Ibid.

56 Ibid.

57 Mackie Rooney, *Margaret Skinnider: 1916 Heroine; The Monaghan Connection*, (Monaghan, 2016), p. 20.

58 Information on Skinnider's teaching career from the Private Archives of her grand-niece, Janet Wilkinson, Australia. Used with permission.

59 Stephen Coyle, talk, 24 Apr. 2014 entitled *No Ordinary Women: The Untold Story of Cumann na mBan in Scotland* https://irishvolunteers.org/report-of-cumann-na-mban-talk-in-glasgow/ accessed 05/01/2019.

60 Margaret Skinnider Military Pension Application File, MSP34REF19910.

61 Ibid.

62 Ibid.

63 Ibid.

Chapter 4

1 They first lived at 31 Waverley Avenue, Fairview, later at 69 Seafield Road, Clontarf, and then, for most of their lives together, they lived at 134 Seafield Road, Clontarf. After Nóra O'Keeffe died (1961) Margaret lived with her sisters and brothers in Clontarf, and in her final years, in Glenageary, County Dublin.

2 O'Keeffe Family Archive, private notes given to the author by Robert O'Keeffe, grandnephew of Nóra O'Keeffe. Eulogy paid to Dan O'Keeffe of Glenough, County Tipperary. Used with permission.

3 BMH WS 1,348, Michael Davern, Officer Commanding (O/C), Tipperary 3rd Brigade, 1920-1921, IRA, p. 20.

4 O'Keeffe Family Archive.

5 Desmond Ryan, *Seán Treacy and the 3rd Tipperary Brigade* (Tralee, 1945), p. 150.

6 Ibid.

7 Ibid., p. 186. This is now St Bricin's Military Hospital in Stoneybatter.

8 Ibid. p.186.

9 Margaret Skinnider, Military Pension Application File, MSP34REF1991.

10 Ibid., Kathleen Clarke wrote a letter of reference for Skinnider which details this work. The 'Dependents' Fund' was the common term for the Irish National Aid Association and Volunteer Dependents' Fund (INAAVDF), which Skinnider had also fund-raised for in America.

11 Letter from Denis O'Keeffe (Fr Benedict) to his brother Michael with the news that the old family home had been blown up. https://www.wikitree.com/wiki/O'Keeffe-252 O'Keeffe Papers, accessed 28/03/2019.

12 Letter from Margaret O'Keeffe (Sr Margaret Mary) to her uncle Michael while she was at home in Glenough in August 1921. https://www.wikitree.com/wiki/O'Keeffe-252 O'Keeffe papers, accessed 28/03/2019

13 BMH WS 1,348, Michael Davern, p. 55.

14 Kathleen Clarke, reference letter, MSP34REF19910.

15 *Freeman's Journal*, Wed., 12 Oct. 1921, p. 4.

16 *The Scotsman*, 13 Oct. 1921, p. 3.

17 *Freeman's Journal*, Mon., 17 Oct. 1921, p. 4.

18 *The Weekly Freeman*, Glasgow, Sat., 28 Oct. 1921, p. 7.

19 National Archives of the United Kingdom, War Office (WO), 35/91/12.

20 Ibid.

21 Lil Conlin, *Cumann na mBan and the Women of Ireland, 1913–25* (Kilkenny, 1969), p. 224.
22 Justin Dolan Stover, 'Families, vulnerability and sexual violence during the Irish Revolution', in Jennifer Evans and Ciara Meehan (eds), *Perceptions of Pregnancy from the Seventeenth to the Twentieth Century* (London, 2017), p. 62.
23 Cal McCarthy, *Cumann na mBan and the Irish Revolution* (Cork, 2007), p. 185.
24 Margaret Ward, *Unmanageable Revolutionaries: Women and Irish* Nationalism (Dublin, 1983), p. 172.
26 Mary McAuliffe 'An idea has gone abroad that all the women were against the Treaty': Cumann na Saoirse and pro-Treaty Women, 1922–1923', in Mícheál Ó Fathartaigh and Liam Weeks (eds), *The Treaty: Debating and Establishing the Irish State* (Dublin, 2018), p. 163.
26 Ibid., p. 168.

Chapter 5

1   Margaret Skinnider, Military Pension Application File, MSP34REF19910, Kathleen Clarke reference letter.
2   MSP34REF19910, Skinnider interview.
3   Ibid.
4   Ibid.
5   Eithne Coyle Papers (UCD Archives), p. 61/4/(68), undated, Cumann na mBan, Anne Delvin Branch, Glasgow.
6   *The Nationalist (Tipperary)*, Sat., 24 May 1969, p. 4.
7   Mary McAuliffe blog, 'Remembering Caitlín Brugha, TD for Waterford, 1923–1927'. https://marymcauliffe.blog/2018/12/04/remembering-caitlin-brugha-td-for-waterford-1923-1927/ accessed 06/07/1019.
8   MSP34REF19910, Skinnider interview.
9   Ibid.
10 Ibid.
11 Austin Stack Papers, National Library of Ireland (NLI), MS 22,3989 (9).
12 Home Office Papers, Brigadier O/C Scotland to QMG, IRA, Dublin HO 144/3746.
13 Ibid.
14 Military Service Pension Application, Nóra/Nan O'Keeffe (neé Walsh), MSP34REF5678.
15 Ibid.
16 With thanks to Claire Guerin for this information on Nóra O'Keeffe from her MPhil thesis (UCC, 2016), 'Anti-Treaty press and publicity in Ireland, 1922–23'.
17 Séumas Robinson, BMH, WS 1721.
18 Charlotte Fallon, 'Civil War hunger strikes: Women and men', in *Éire*, vol. 22 (1987), p. 83.
19 Ibid.
20 McCarthy, *Cumann na mBan*, pp 222–3.
21 Margaret Buckley, *Jangle of the Keys* (Dublin, 1938), p. 31.

22 Kilmainham Archives, *Éire/ Irish Nation*, 7 Apr. 1923, p. 4. *Éire/ Irish Nation* printed in Glasgow, it was edited and proofread by the Glasgow Anne Devlin Cumann na mBan women. It was sold by selected agents and by Cumann na mBan women in Ireland. It was put on a banned list of publications by the Free State authorities and anyone in procession of a copy could be arrested.

23 Ibid.

24 Ibid.

25 Annie O'Farrelly Papers, National Library of Ireland (NLI), MS47, 640/21, 8 May 1923.

26 Ibid.

27 Ibid.

28 Ibid.

29 Prison Journal of Cecilia Saunders Gallagher, 20 Sept. 1923, Trinity College Dublin, Manuscripts. IE TCD MS10056.

30 Hannah Moynihan, Prison Diary, 1 May 1923, KGMA (2010), 1246.

31 Margaret Ward, *Unmanageable Revolutionaries: Women and Irish* Nationalism (Dublin, 1983), p. 194.

32 Laura McAtackney, 'Gender, incarceration and power relations during the Irish Civil War, 1922–1923', in Victoria Sanford, Katerina Stefatos and Cecilia M. Salvi (eds), *Gender Violence in Peace and War: States of Complicity* (Toronto, 2016), p. 58.

33 O'Farrelly Papers, MS47, 640/21.

34 Ibid.

35 Buckley, *Jangle of the Keys*, pp 59–61.

36 O'Farrelly Papers, MS47, 640/21, 12 July 1923.

37 '"Blaze away with you little guns": A memoir of three jails; Tralee, Kilmainham and the North Dublin Union' by 'Two of them' (Cis and Jo Power), KMGA (2010), 0247-49, Box 4.

38 Moynihan, Prison Diary, Mon., 11 June 1923, KMGA, 2010.1246.

39 Ibid., Sun., 18 July 1923.

40 O'Farrelly Papers, MS47, 640/21, 12 July 1923.

41 *Irish Nation (Éire)*, 5 Aug. 1923.

42 Ann Mathews, *Dissents: Irish Republican Women, 1923–1941* (Cork, 2012), p. 109.

43 Sheehy Skeffington Papers, NLI MS, 41,178 (31). Letter from Nora Connolly to Hanna Sheehy Skeffington,4 Oct. 1923.

44 Ibid., p. 110.

Chapter 6

1 Maryann Gialanella Valiulis, 'Virtuous mothers and dutiful wives: The politics of sexuality in the Irish Free State', in Maryann Gialanella Valiulis (ed.), *Gender and Power in Irish History* (Dublin, 2009), p. 134.

2 See Mary McAuliffe '"The unquiet sisters": Women, politics and the Irish Free State Senate 1922–1936', in Clara Fischer and Mary McAuliffe (eds), *Irish Feminisms: Past, Present and Future* (Dublin, 2015), p. 50.

3   Markievicz was elected as a Fianna Fáil TD in June 1927 and she may have taken her seat along with the other Fianna Fáil TDs, but she died, unexpectedly, in July 1927.

4   Mary Clancy, 'Aspects of women's contribution to the Oireachtas debate in the Irish Free State, 1922–1937', in Maria Luddy & Cliona Murphy (eds), *Women Surviving: Studies in Irish women's History in the 19th and 20th centuries* (Dublin, 1990), p. 217.

5   These were Jennie Wyse Power, Eileen Costello, Kathleen Clarke, Kathleen Browne, Alice Stopford Green. The sixth was the Countess of Desart.

6   Mary McAuliffe, 'An idea has gone abroad that all the women were against the Treaty': Cumann na Saoirse and pro-Treaty Women, 1922–1923', in Mícheál Ó Fathartaigh and Liam Weeks (eds), *The Treaty: Debating and Establishing the Irish State* (Dublin, 2018), p. 179.

7   McAuliffe 'The unquiet sisters', p. 50.

8   Eoin O'Leary, 'The Irish National Teachers' Organisation and the Marriage Bar for women national teachers, 1933–1958', in *Saothar* 12 (1987), p. 49.

9   Ibid., p. 50.

10 Margaret Ward, *Unmanageable Revolutionaries: Women and Irish Nationalism* (Dublin, 1983), p. 199.

11 Sheehy Skeffington Manuscripts, NLI, MS 33,606/11, Nóra O'Keeffe to Hanna Sheehy Skeffington, 29 Jan. 1924.

12 Sheehy Skeffington Manuscripts, NLI, MS 41,178/34, Nóra O'Keeffe to Hanna Sheehy Skeffington, undated, 1924.

13 Sheehy Skeffington Manuscripts, NLI MS 41,178/40, Margaret Skinnider to Hanna Sheehy Skeffington, 8 July 1924.

14 Sheehy Skeffington Manuscripts, NLI MS 41,178/44, Margaret Skinnider to Hanna Sheehy Skeffington, 31 Mar. 1926.

15 Sheehy Skeffington Manuscripts, NLI MS 41,178/97 Nóra O'Keeffe to Hanna Sheehy Skeffington, 3 June 1937.

16 Sheehy Skeffington Manuscripts, NLI MS 41,178/70, Margaret Skinnider to Hanna Sheehy Skeffington, 14 Feb. 1931.

17 Sheehy Skeffington Manuscripts, NLI, MS 41,178/81, Nóra O'Keeffe to Hanna Sheehy Skeffington, 1933.

18 Marie Coleman, 'Military service pensions and the recognition and reintegration of guerrilla fighters after the Irish revolution', in *Historical Research*, vol. 91:253 (2018), pp 554–72, Abstract.

19 Ibid. p. 556.

20 Marie Coleman, 'Compensating Irish female revolutionaries, 1916–1923', in *Women's History Review*, vol. 26, Extract 6 (2017), p. 920.

21 Dáil Debates, vol. 8 (15 July 1924), col. 1266.

22 *The Irish Times*, 1 Jan. 1923, p. 5.

23 See Louise Ryan, 'Splendidly silent: Representing Irish republican women, 1919–23', in Lubelska Gallagher and Louise Ryan (eds), *Re-presenting the Past: Women and History* (London, 2001), pp 23–43 for representations of pro and anti-Treaty women in the press.

24 Margaret Skinnider, MSPC 1925, W1P724.

25 Ibid.
26 Ibid.
27 Ibid.
28 Treasury Solicitor to Army Finance Officer, 18 Mar. 1925, MSPC, W1P724.
29 Skinnider to Army Pensions Dept. 8 Sept. 1927, MSPC, W1P724.
30 Army Pensions Branch to Skinnider, 9 Sept. 1927, MSPC, W1P724.
31 Bríd Connolly, MSPC, MSP34REF3977. Thanks to Dr John Borgonovo, UCC, for this reference.
32 Coleman, 'Compensating Irish female revolutionaries', p. 923.
33 Ibid.
34 Ibid.
35 Margaret Ward (ed.), *In Their Own Voice: Women and Irish Nationalism* (Cork, 2001), p. 169–70.
36 Cumann na mBan Convention Minutes, 15 Nov. 1925, UCDAD, Humphreys Papers, p106/1136 (6).
37 Ibid., p. 10.
38 Cumann na mBan Executive Meeting, 19 Sept. 1924, UCDAD, Humphreys Papers, p106/1105.
39 Cumann na mBan, Annual Convention document, 15 Nov. 1925, UCDAD, MacSwiney Papers, 48a/15, p. 7.
40 Cumann na mBan Convention Minutes, 15 Nov. 1925, UCDAD, Humphreys Papers, p106/1136 (12).
41 Cumann na mBan Executive Meeting, 17 Dec. 1925, UCDAD, Humphreys Papers, p106/1107.
42 Ibid.
43 Emmet O'Connor, 'The Socialist Party of Ireland', in D. George Boyce and Alan O'Day (eds), *Ireland in Transition, 1867–1921* (London, 2004), p. 231.
44 *The Irish Citizen*, April–May 1920, p. 83.
45 *The Leitrim Observer*, Sat., 20 Mar. 1926, p. 4.
46 Ann Mathews, *Dissents: Irish Republican Women, 1923–1941* (Cork, 2012), pp 298–304.
47 Sheehy Skeffington Manuscripts, NLI, MS 41,178 /99, Kathleen Clarke to Hanna Sheehy Skeffington, 18 June 1937.
48 Sheehy Skeffington Manuscripts, NLI, MS 41,178 /99, Nóra O'Keeffe to Hanna Sheehy Skeffington, 3 June 1937.
49 *Prison Bars*, July 1937, in Ward, *In Their Own Voice*, p. 184.

Chapter 7

1 John Coolahan, *Irish Education: Its History and Structure* (Dublin, 1981), p. 31.
2 Síle Chuinneagáin, *Catherine Mahon: First President of the INTO* (Dublin, 1998), p. 14.
3 Eoin O'Leary, 'The Irish National Teachers' Organisation and the Marriage Bar for women national teachers, 1933–1958', in *Saothar*, vol. 12 (1987), p. 47.

4   Ibid.
5   Ibid.
6   Niamh Puirséil, *Kindling the Flame: 150 Years of the Irish National Teachers' Organisation* (Dublin, 2017), p. 88.
7   *Irish School Weekly (ISW)*, 1 Oct. 1938.
8   Puirséil, *Kindling the Flame*, p. 89.
9   Eugene McCormick, *The INTO and the 1946 Teachers' Strike* (Dublin, 1996), p. 13.
10 Ibid., p. 14
11 Senate Debates, vol. 31 (21 Mar. 1946), p. 1,046.
12 McCormick, *The INTO and the 1946 Teachers' Strike*, pp 24–5.
13 Ibid., p. 28.
14 Ibid., p. 38.
15 Ibid.
16 *The Irish Times*, Editorial, 30 Oct. 1946.
17 Eithne Mac Dermott, *Clann na Poblachta* (Cork, 1998), p. 13.
18 Ibid., p. 34.
19 *The Irish Independent*, Wed., 8 Oct. 1947, p. 5.
20 Ibid., p. 37
21 Puirséil, *Kindling the Flame*, p. 117.
22 Ibid., p. 119
23 *The Irish Press*, 28 Dec.1956.
24 *The Irish Independent*, 13 May 1953, p. 7.
25 Mackie Rooney, *Margaret Skinnider: 1916 Heroine; The Monaghan Connection* (Monaghan, 2016), p. 29
26 *The Irish Independent*, Fri., 6 Apr. 1956, p. 8.
27 Rooney, *Margaret Skinnider*, p. 31.
28 *The Irish Examiner*, 23 Apr. 1956.
29 Ibid.
30 Ibid.
31 Yvonne Galligan, *Women and Politics in Contemporary Ireland: From the Margins to the Mainstream* (Dublin, 1998).
32 *The Irish Times*, 22 July 1963, p. 7
33 Ibid., 20 Apr. 1964.
34 Ibid.
35 Ibid.
36 I would particularly like to thank Margaret Skinnider's grandniece, Janet Wilkinson, who kindly allowed me access to all the many wonderful photographs which she inherited from Margaret. These photos are a detailed treasure trove of Margaret and Nóra's life together.
37 *The Irish Examiner*, 15 Aug. 1961, p. 7.
38 *The Irish Independent*, Wed., 12 Aug. 1964, p. 20.
39 *The Irish Examiner*, Tues., 12 Oct. 1971, p. 16.

Conclusion

1 Eithne Coyle, Lecture in University College Dublin, UCDA, Sighle Humphreys Papers, quoted in Senia Pašeta, *Irish Nationalist Women, 1900–1918* (Cambridge, 2013), p. 1.

2 Fearghal McGarry, '"Too many histories?" The Bureau of Military History and Easter 1916', in *History Ireland* vol. 19, no. 6 (Nov./Dec. 2011), p. 28.

3 The *Irish Times*, 17 Jan. 2014, p. 1.

4 Ibid., Fintan O'Toole '1916: Portraits and lives', edited by Lawrence William White and James Quinn, Sat., 10 Oct. 2015.

5 Photographs and artefacts not seen in years were loaned to the exhibition by Skinnider's grandniece, Janet Wilkinson.

6 The Margaret Skinnider Appreciation Society continues in existence. The Society were of great help in researching the Monaghan connections for this book. I am deeply grateful for their hospitality and for sharing their knowledge of the Monaghan side of the Skinnider family story.

7 Kirsty Lusk and Willy Maley (eds), *Scotland and the Easter Rising; Fresh Perspectives on 1916* (Edinburgh, 1916); and Stephen Coyle and Máirtín Ó Catháin '*We Will Rise Again: Ireland, Scotland and the Easter Rising* (Glasgow, 2018); as well as Rooney, *Margaret Skinnider: 1916 Heroine. Doing My Bit for Ireland* (Edinburgh, 2016) was re-issued, with an introduction by Kirsty Lusk.

8 Rooney, *Margaret Skinnider*, p. 75.

9 Ibid.

10 Ibid.

11 *An Múinteoir Naisúnta*, Bealtaine (May 1966), p. 22.

12 Piaras Béaslaí Papers, NLI Ms 33,912 (8).

13 Ibid.

14 https://www.independent.ie/irish-news/1916/audio-and-video/listen-to-stories-from-1916-margaret-skinnider-the-rebels-sniper-34540910.html accessed 09/03/2019.

15 *The Irish Independent*, 30 Sept. 1963.

Select Bibliographical Details

Primary Sources

Skinnider's own work, *Doing My Bit for Ireland* (New York, 1917), introduces her early life path towards, and involvement in, the 1916 Rising. The records of political women held in the National Library of Ireland (NLI) and in UCD Archives proved invaluable, both for Margaret Skinnider and for Nóra O'Keeffe. These included the Sheehy Skeffington Manuscripts in the NLI, as well as the Annie O'Farrelly, Rosamond Jacob, Austin Stack, and Piaras Beaslaí Papers held in that Library. At the UCD Archives records on Cumann na mBan, particularly in the post-1923 period, can be found among the Sighle Humphreys, Eithne Coyle, Máire Comerford, and Mary MacSwiney papers, while the Patricia Coughlan papers were useful for Clann na Poblachta. In the Kilmainham Jail Archives, the Moynihan sisters' diaries and the Power sisters' memoirs were invaluable, as was the prison journal of Cecilia Saunders Gallagher, held in Trinity College Dublin. The Military Archives, which hold the Military Pension Application files and the Bureau of Military History Witness Statements, among other resources, have been a boon for any historian of Irish revolutionary women, proven again in this work. Sources for Skinnider's career in the INTO can be found in the INTO archives, in the pages of the *Irish School Weekly* and in the national newspapers. The privately held family archives for both Skinnider and O'Keeffe, which were kindly shared by their families, were also essential. Republican, Scottish, Irish and international newspapers provided extra detail on the life and work of Margaret Skinnider, and the organisations of which she was part. The work of the Margaret Skinnider Appreciation Society in Monaghan and their publication, written by Mackie Rooney, *Margaret Skinnider, 1916 Heroine; The Monaghan Connection* (2016) showed the importance of her Monaghan ancestry in the development of her nationalist ideology.

Scottish Sources

There were several publications in 2016 which reflected on and commemorated the part played by the Irish emigrant population in Scotland in the revolutionary decade in Ireland. These were a very useful introduction to Skinnider's early history and the important connections between suffrage, nationalist and socialist politics in Ireland and in Scotland. These include Helen Crawfurd's unpublished diaries, as well as publications such as Kirsty Lusk and Willy Maley (eds), *Scotland and the Easter Rising* (Edinburgh, 2016); Stephen Coyle and Máirtín Ó Catháin (eds), *We Will Rise Again: Ireland, Scotland and the Easter Rising* ((Glasgow, 2018) Looking at suffrage in Britain, Elizabeth Crawford's *The Women's Suffrage Movement: A Reference Guide, 1866–1928* (London, 2001) was a very useful starting point. Other books which revealed the militant history of the Scottish suffragettes included Sarah Pedersen, *The Scottish Suffragettes and the Press* (London, 2017) and Leah Leneman's *A Guid Cause: The Women's Suffrage Movement in Scotland* (Edinburgh, 1995), Iain McLean's *The Legend of Red Clydeside* (Edinburgh, 1983) also proved very illuminating on the history of radical politics in early twentieth-century Glasgow.

Suffrage and Revolutionary Women

Among the books consulted for this study were Margaret Ward's groundbreaking book, *Unmanageable Revolutionaries: Women and Irish Nationalism* (London, 1983) and *In Their Own Voice: Women and Irish Nationalism* (Dublin, 1989); for a history of Irish suffrage activism Rosemary Cullen Owens's *Smashing Times: A History of the Irish Women's Suffrage Movement 1889–1922* (Dublin, 1984); while Mary Jones's *Those Obstreperous Lassies: A History of the IWWU* (Dublin, 1988) looks at the working-class women of the trade unions. The women of Cumann na mBan are well served by Louise Ryan and Margaret Ward (eds), *Irish Women and Nationalism: Soldiers, New Women and Wicked Hags* (Dublin, 2004); Cal MacCarthy's *Cumann na mBan and the Irish Revolution* (Cork, 2007); Ann Mathews's *Renegades: Irish Republican Women 1900–1922* (Dublin, 2010) and *Dissidents: Irish Republican Women 1923–1941* (Dublin, 2012); Joanne Mooney Eichacker, *Irish Republican Women in America: Lecture Tour, 1916–1925* (Dublin, 2003). As 2016 approached several critically well received books dealing with women, nationalism and revolution were published, including Senia Pašeta's *Irish Nationalist Women, 1900–1918* (Cambridge, 2013); Lucy McDiarmid *At Home in the Revolution: What Women Said and Did In 1916* (Dublin, 2015); Sinéad McCoole, *Easter Widows* and *Rebel Sisters* (Dublin, 2014); and Mary McAuliffe and Liz Gilles', *Richmond Barracks; We Were There: 77 Women of the Easter Rising* (Dublin, 2016).

Twentieth-Century Ireland

Margaret Skinnider lived until 1971, almost 50 years after the founding of the Irish Free State. Works which proved important in researching and writing the later part of her life were Niamh Puirséil, *Kindling the Flame: 150 Years of the Irish National Teachers' Organisation* (Dublin, 2017); Eithne Mac Dermott, *Clann na Poblachta* (Cork, 1998); Kevin Rafter, *The Clann: The Story of Clann Na Poblachta* (Dublin, 1996); John Coolahan, *Irish Education: Its History and Structure* (Dublin, 1981). Rosemary Cullen Owens's *A Social History of Women in Ireland, 1870–1970* (Dublin, 2007) provided a social, cultural and political context. Recent publications which broaden our knowledge of the histories and biographies of activist women include: Leeann Lane, *Rosamond Jacob: Third Person Singular* (Dublin, 2010); Clara Fischer and Mary McAuliffe (eds), *Irish Feminisms: Past, Present, and Future* (Dublin, 2015); and Margaret Ward, *Hanna Sheehy Skeffington: Suffragette and Sinn Féiner; Her Memoirs and Political Writings* (Dublin 2017).

Index